With Duncan Grant in
Southern Turkey

Books by Paul Roche

The Rat and the Convent Dove
O Pale Galilean
All Things Considered
To Tell the Truth
New Tales from Aesop

FRONTISPIECE: *Still Life with Matisse*,
painted 1971.
Acquired by Her Majesty Queen Elizabeth
the Queen Mother in 1973 at the opening
of Duncan Grant's exhibition at the
Fermoy Gallery in King's Lynn.

With Duncan Grant in Southern Turkey

Paul Roche

Honeyglen Publishing

First published in Great Britain by Honeyglen
Publishing Limited in 1982.

British Library Cataloguing in Publication Data
Roche, Paul
With Duncan Grant in Southern Turkey.
1. Grant, Duncan
 I. Title
759.2   ND497.D/

ISBN 0 907855 00 8

Printed and bound in Great Britain by
Robert MacLehose and Co. Ltd.
Renfrew, Scotland.

To Angelica Garnett

CONTENTS

The author wishes to thank the Marguerite
Eyer Wilbur Foundation, with whose help the
book was completed.

The author and publishers also wish to thank
Ronald Alley and Richard Shone for their
advice on the selection of the paintings;
the designer, John Munday;
the copy-editor, Sue Phillpott;
and Mrs Erma Bigland.

For permission to reproduce paintings from their collections the author and publishers wish to thank:

Her Majesty Queen Elizabeth the Queen Mother	*Still Life with Matisse*	frontispiece
		facing page
Angelica Garnett	*The Tub*	56
The Tate Gallery	*Bathing*	41
	Girl at the Piano	57
The National Portrait Gallery	*Self-portrait*	40
Pandora Smith	*The Turkish Café*	105
And from the collection of the author	*Hayfield*	88
	Poppies	89
	Portrait of Paul Roche	104

Derry Moore for the photograph of Duncan Grant and Paul Roche on jacket front.

The Tate Gallery for permission to reproduce *The Queen of Sheba* on jacket back.

Introduction

It is nearly thirty-six years since I first met Duncan – a warm night off Piccadilly – and when he said to me: 'Would you like to see some pictures?' I was so green, so unevolved, that I thought he meant films, movies. 'Why not?' I said.

We put my bicycle on a taxi-cab – it was the old sort of cab, capacious enough for anything – and drove to Edward le Bas' house in Bedford Square, where Duncan stayed during and soon after the war whenever he came to London.

A great part of Edward's collection of contemporary English painting, which was to become famous, already hung from the walls. With half a tumbler each of very cheap rum in our hands – the only thing we could get – we went the rounds, and I met eye-on for the first time such painters as Sickert, Harold Gilman, Charles Ginner, Mark Gertler, Augustus John (and Gwen), Paul Nash, Matthew Smith and Vanessa Bell. With the modesty I did not then know was characteristic of him, Duncan kept his own work till last. By then the rum was having its effect and his painting of a white handkerchief with coloured borders, half spread out next to a glass cheese-dish – though I said I liked it more than a lot of the other pictures – hardly dazzled my ignorant eye. I collapsed on a sofa, collapsed with laughter at Sickert's girl with the black-brimmed hat smiling across at me, and said she looked like a monkey. Duncan, by no means unmerry but a little nonplussed at my lack of finesse, then showed me his drawing for the book-jacket of Arthur Waley's *Monkey*, and I saw for the first time how witty and delicate a design could be. When he asked me if I would sit for him the next day, vanity and curiosity made me say yes.

So began my first eight years of almost continuous modelling and sitting for Duncan. And so began too the education of my eye. I went with him to the Tate and the National Galleries. I went with him to every show at the Leicester Galleries, Agnews, the Adams brothers, the Lefevre and elsewhere. I watched him paint six sketches of St Paul's from new vistas opened up by the great blitz. And when he showed me the final picture – commissioned by the Queen (our present Queen Mother) – something began to dawn in my eye and my brain.

It was several years before I knew what that something was, but the finished

1

painting of St Paul's – a largish picture of about 5 ft × 3 ft – held me: its tightness and completeness yet liveliness and luminosity. Everything I had missed in the sketches I now saw in them too and I caught an inkling of how Duncan achieved his amazing unity. He attacked the whole as a whole on the first onslaught. His pictures grew like eggs: the entire embryo was there at the moment of conception.

It is true that during our sittings I continued to plague him to 'finish' his drawings and paintings of me, and he continued to reply: 'Some people think that a work which is any good is "finished", as you say, with the first few strokes.' I mused on this and also wondered what he meant by the phrase 'pure colour'. Vanessa Bell, he said, was the purest colourist he knew. Then he gave me my first picture: the painting of a dead duck hanging by its broken neck. I thought to myself: 'Why does he have to be so ruthlessly uncompromising in his choice of subject? And why so disconcerting some-times in his composition?' By which I meant the choice and arrangement of objects, not what he meant – the choice and arrangement of paint.

Then I began to notice something. Duncan, even when being wilful and 'disconcer-ting' (which I put down partly to his Scots ancestry), could fill half a canvas with a blank wall or a flat expanse of door and still make it sing. My eye, brought up to look only for verisimilitude, was surprised to find that within the representation of reality a tune was being played, a wonderfully orchestrated melody of vibrations which had nothing to do – and everything to do – with making a thing look real. Not a brush-stroke of Duncan's blank wall but it was a note in a rigorously integrated chromatic scale. Not a patch of colour in one corner but it was related in tone throughout the whole canvas to a patch of colour in another. I still did not know what tune it was, but I knew now that Duncan's determination not to please except by telling the truth, and telling the truth through the intransigent beauty of paint, was working magic on me; at least on my second glance. I could take any one of his pictures – even the dead duck – turn it upside down, isolate six square inches anywhere, look at it with fervent scrutiny and hear, or rather see, a small separate melody . . . The isolated portion, cut off from the rest of the picture and from all it needed to make it real, nevertheless went on pulsing with its own life. A whole design on its own – a whole abstract painting, if you like – played out its lively little dance within the larger composition. That is what I saw. I began to understand why Duncan's work grew on me.

It was then that certain critics perplexed me. 'Duncan Grant?' they said. 'Ah, yes, look at his early work. That is his best.' I went back to the Tate and gazed at his portrait of James Strachey, a very early work with the full glow of his first visit to Italy upon it – when he studied Giotto and Paolo Veronese and copied the Masaccios in the Church of the Carmine in Florence. 'Oh yes, remarkable,' they said, 'but too early. We meant the work he did after the great Post-Impressionist show at the Grafton Gallery in 1910.'

I visited Charleston, where Clive and Vanessa Bell had been living with Duncan since the First War; dug out canvas after musty canvas dating from 1910 to about 1925; saw in them the gay, marvellously inventive evocation of a Cézanne turning into a Matisse; saw, too, that the young Duncan Grant had added a lyrical English unexpectedness, an almost Elizabethan freshness of imagination, to his 'uncle' Matisse. No wonder they had called him in the Twenties 'the Matisse of England'.

I looked at these early works and loved them – as who could not? They gave immediate pleasure, but did they really face the problem of telling the truth? What the critics had said failed to convince me. His best work? Surely not. Certainly not his most serious. Was it conceivable that when Duncan had stopped painting in this often fanciful, always fetching, idiom the critics had stopped looking? New stars were on the horizon: Graham Sutherland, Francis Bacon. Perhaps there was not, nor was it, the time to see what I saw as I gazed deeper into Duncan's works from about 1938 onwards. An extraordinary transformation, slow and often painful, was taking place: Duncan Grant was growing into a great painter. A seemingly impossible goal began to reveal itself: one towards which he was now pushing painting after painting.

I took to scrutinising those very canvases which critics had been half-hearted about, had even called dull, muddy, academic. Here was a coffee-pot, here an opulent cluster of oriental poppies in a heavy jar, here a dead pheasant hanging. Yes, they looked almost academic at first sight: they were such tight and complete representations of the real world. But why was it that after a few minutes they filled the room with their presence, and that after a week (if I was lucky enough to have them hanging on my walls) I could not on my life be parted from them? This was not the way of 'academic' pictures, which, after a tolerable first glance, regressed steadily in the direction of boredom. Why did a coffee-pot by Duncan Grant, which by no means knocked me out on the first glance, begin to bewitch on the second, cast a definite spell on the third, and hold me in thraldom for life on the twenty-fifth?

I came up to his canvases with a microscope – by which I mean a large magnifying-glass – and what I beheld was this: Duncan was pure Cézanne, but a Cézanne pushed to such a minute mastery of representational truth that the very process of it was undetectable to the conscious eye: that eye which does not see everything and notices only something. These pictures were indeed the painting of the real world over again, 'but this time from nature', which Cézanne had devoutly expressed as his ultimate wish. They were aspiring to the truth and the solidity of a Chardin, but a Chardin only Cézanne could have painted.

When I tried to analyse what I had discovered, I could not deny that the whole amazing balancing-act of relating volume to weight to plasticity to roundness to distance to projection into certain dimensions of space, was being perfected through line, tone and colour *within* the very counterpoint of a separate melody. Reality was captured, oh yes, but in the very act the whole scale of flat patterns Cézanne had invented was given a new set of rhythms, and new vibrations. So miraculously resolved were these that they remained hidden persuaders, available only to the sub-conscious eye: that eye which sees everything and notices nothing. The swift perception of similarities that had charmed everyone in Duncan Grant's early work, was now turned into a passionate observance of the object itself. The act of contemplation and the vision themselves became the music. And the thrill was hidden in the act of recognition.

> That was why
> The most bovine eye
> Was caught in the end
> By the very paintings
> The critics had passed by.

I realised with a kind of horror the enormous risk Duncan had run and what had been the struggle. No painter myself, I had once had the impertinence to paint a picture of a straw-covered Chianti bottle next to a lemon and an egg, with Duncan and Edward le Bas (an Academician at that!) in the same room, both drawing me painting. Such was my concentration that I finished my picture in twenty minutes, and I was dripping with sweat. To focus a passionate observance on the object is to put oneself in danger of being tyrannised by it, and to be tyrannised by the object is to be impotent when it comes to saying anything about it in paint. I had said nothing about my Chianti bottle, lemon and egg, but they looked almost real. The picture was a fraud. We laughed . . . Duncan on the other hand had faced his enormous ordeal: the dual responsibility in every brush-stroke of being true to the object and true to his aesthetic principles of composition. He was painting pictures which mastered the appearances of reality without ever submerging the values of paint as paint under the dictates of verisimilitude. I was stunned.

During these years, 1946 to 1954, I shared a flat at no. 1 Taviton Street, Bloomsbury, with Marjorie Strachey, Lytton's sister and Duncan's cousin. I occupied a small room hung from top to bottom with Duncan's drawings and paintings. It was while letting my eyes dwell, one summer afternoon, on a small picture of a Sussex haystack above my bed, and wishing I were in a field near Charleston rather than in London, that I realised something else about Duncan's work which I had never heard anybody say. Duncan, by dint of getting me to look, had given me a love of Constable, and I knew that Constable no less than Chardin was one of his heroes. Now, while lazily peering at this haystack, from which I could almost smell the warm mustiness of a drowsy afternoon and hear the bluebottles in the tall heavy lace of the elms, I began to remember what Duncan had told me about Constable: how he had got away from the conventional painting of the early nineteenth century and walked out of the studios and the drawing-rooms into the open – to look at nature with fresh and utterly honest eyes. And also, how he had faced the problem of light: light among woods and fields,

4

light among clouds, light on water. Then I remembered that when Constable was seen by the French for the first time it was to them an eye-opener. Delacroix professed himself bowled over. His enthusiasm for this new approach to nature out of doors, this new fidelity to water and clouds and light, spread to others and eventually led to the Impressionists and after them to Cézanne.

On that afternoon, looking at Duncan's Sussex haystack, the truth hit me. This was pure Constable – the scene and the spirit could only be English – but a Constable that had gone through France, run the gamut of the Impressionists and then Cézanne, and come back to England. Was this not a remarkable thing to have done? Nobody else, so far as I knew, had such a title to fame. However, I kept my theories to myself, or aired them only to such of my friends who knew nothing of Bloomsbury. When I showed off my collection to them at Taviton Street, I used to carry out what I called 'the Velazquez test'. This involved propping up a mirror in the bathroom and then standing at an angle in the corridor with one of Duncan's pictures (the only possible way in my small quarters of getting the required distance) and arranging the reflection so to be given by the mirror that the picture seemed actually to be framed in the mirror. Then I would watch the astonishment of my viewers, who stood in the corridor. The bowl of roses or the hanging pheasant or the dish of fruit were no longer paintings: they were real. The mass of brush-strokes that had seemed incoherent in their simplicity when seen close up, fell miraculously into the contours of something humming with its own being and essence. If it was a landscape I held up towards the mirror, then the mirror changed into a window out of which one looked at a vignette of real woods and fields and sky: a superb piece of painting revealed – with all the definition of a Velazquez. An ordinary picture remained an ordinary picture seen in a mirror. Not many painters, I found, could withstand the Velazquez test. Duncan did.

It was in 1961, soon after Vanessa's death that – leaving my wife and young family in Mexico and coming back to England after eight years abroad – I found myself again at Charleston. It was a morning in August, Duncan had gone to Lewes and I thought myself alone except for Grace his devoted housekeeper and Walter her husband (who helped to tend the garden), when the studio door opened and in walked Clive. I had forgotten he was in the house. He rarely ventured into any of the studios. I think it was an understood thing that Clive Bell, the art critic, must keep himself professionally detached from the two painters living on the spot. Clive, walking very slowly across the studio floor (he was over eighty and this was one of the last two summers left to him) and excusing his intrusion by saying he was taking the shortest way to see if there were any ripe figs on the trees in Duncan's patio, suddenly stood stock still. He did not know that the task I had set myself during Duncan's absence was to comb through the three studios and select six of the best pictures that, in my judgment, Duncan had ever painted. Clive did not move. He looked for a long time, then said: 'I have never seen any of these before. What beauties! Why haven't I seen them at a show? These are some of the best paintings Duncan has ever painted.' My elation knew no bounds. My eye at last, it seemed, was educated. I boasted of it to Duncan when he came home — and for years afterwards.

On January 21st 1978 Duncan entered the threshold of his ninety-fourth year. Since 1961 he had, to my mind, painted many pictures as fine as — and some finer than — those exquisite six Clive stumbled on that August morning on his way to the figs. He had triumphed in reaching the almost impossible goal he set himself. After Cézanne there could be only two directions to go in (within that tradition): one was to break down still further his rhythm of flat patterns into ever larger and simpler units: the way of Matisse. The other was to see how far they could be brought together, resolved: the way of Duncan Grant. He had pushed Cézanne's insistence on design within the realistic structure of painting, to such subtleties, simplicities and densities of resolution, that of some of his most recent work one might say: only an angel could have painted it. 'Angel' here not connoting something ethereal and remote but an earthy tangible effulgence vibrating with touch, taste, colour, sound and smell . . . If indeed the angels are, as I think, part of that creative consciousness — the ultimate 'nous' of the Greeks — which constitutes the world in being.

Most of this introduction is taken from 'A Personal Appreciation' and 'The Education of an Eye' as published in *Transatlantic Review*, 1975, for permission to use which the author expresses his thanks.

Early in September

Why Turkey? . . . Because it has to be a place where the summer is in full swing. It has to be comparatively near, for I have failed to lure Duncan to Mexico or an island in the Caribbean. When I say to him: 'The trying thing in air travel now is not the distance but getting on to the plane; whether one goes to Paris or Cape Town the process is the same,' he answers: 'The distances are greater.' 'Of course,' I say, 'but one has all the more time to recover in.' To which he murmurs: 'One leaves one's soul behind.'

We consider Rex Nan Kivell's place in Tangier. Duncan has stayed there before. It would be delightful, safety-first and uneventful. He would sketch all day and I would lie in the sun. This seems tame compared to Turkey, of which he knows only Istanbul (and *that* sixty-five years ago), and I know nothing. I suggest a Mediterranean cruise. Certainly not: he has a horror of the sea.

We find ourselves delving into glossy travel brochures on Turkey. We talk 'Turkey' to our friends. Three books on Turkey make their appearance, including Lord Kinross's *Europa Minor* and George Bean's *Turkey's Southern Shore*. I begin to read them out aloud. John Haylock comes to Charleston to tea and extols Side, a Greco-Roman town full of classical nostalgia and of ruins tumbling into the sea. 'You find yourself swimming over a marble column,' he says. 'Now it's a charming ramshackle village.' This sounds just the place for us.

I go to London and call at the Turkish Aegean tourist agents in South Molton Street. Arrangements are under way. I feel elated and slightly guilty because these include the hire of a car and my family has forbidden me to drive. We are to pick it up in Antalya. We are to be gone three weeks.

September 14th and 15th

The equipping of Duncan proves a two-day process: one he enters on with apprehension and I with relish. We leave for Turkey on Sunday the 16th, in the evening, and have come up to London from Aldermaston this morning . . . He needs a light cotton suit, so I take him to C & A in Oxford Street where two years ago he scored a triumph with a lightweight brown suit and another of blue all for £23. This time we go to a different C & A, the one near Oxford Circus. Meanwhile, Potey, my son, who accompanies us with an aloof kind of gangling disdain, floats around the shop marvelling that we should set our sartorial sights no higher than C & A. This branch is certainly not so rich in variety as the one we went to before, and we have problems. The suits Duncan likes, he cannot get into, and the suits he can get into are more expensive and not so well liked. He fancies himself in black velvet. Luckily, this is one of the suits he cannot get into.

* * * * *

'Duncan, when I first met you (that warm July night crossing Piccadilly Circus), you were wearing a hand-tailored suit of chequered tweed. It was new and you said you'd got it to go to Copenhagen in. Round your neck was a black-dotted silk bow-tie, carelessly tied. I thought you looked distinguished and rather wicked.'

'I dare say. And you were dressed in black trousers and a flimsy short-sleeved dark-blue shirt. I thought you looked very young . . . It reminds me a little of when I first met Maynard — though he was only a few years older than me, and I don't think I could have looked as innocent as you.'

'But wasn't Maynard *much* older than you?'

'No, but he acted as though he was.'

'Where did this meeting take place?'

'In London, at a bar: a pub not far from Victoria Station.'

'A pick-up?'

'I suppose you could call it that. Though I already knew him by sight. He came up and said: "Haven't we met before?" '

'And had you?'

'Of course we had. Just vaguely. This time it was a real meeting. I went back with him to his flat — he was living in Victoria Street. I was very dirty and he asked me if I'd like to have a bath.'

'Was that just a gambit to see if you stripped as well as you looked?'

'I think he genuinely thought I had to have a bath. Possibly it was a bit of a gambit too. But I'd come straight from the farm, where I'd been shovelling manure or something — so I was filthy.'

'It was during the First War, then, when you and Bunny Garnett were working on a farm as conscientious objectors?'

'No, long before. It must have been soon after I came back from Paris in 1907, where I'd been living as a student most of the year.'*

---

* Here there has been an obvious telescoping of Duncan's memory.

'And did Maynard see how well you stripped?'

'Yes. He continued his conversation with me on the edge of the bath.'

'You hadn't left Lytton at that stage, had you?'

'No.'

'Did you feel you were being unfaithful to Lytton?'

'Yes, I think I did. I didn't behave very well towards Lytton all those years. I mean about two years after I had met Maynard. I'd known Lytton much longer than that.'

'Of course. When your parents were in India you'd more or less been brought up with the Stracheys – your cousins . . . I remember your telling me something that was related to you afterwards, how when you were about nineteen Lytton came upon you lying asleep on a bed and turned to someone and said: "My God, how beautiful he is!" '

'Yes, I believe something of the sort happened.'

'Well, was Lytton upset when you deserted him for Maynard?'

'I think he was. It made it worse that Lytton was very fond of Maynard. They were great friends at Cambridge, though I don't think it was an affair.'

'Did Maynard and Lytton go on seeing one another?'

'Yes, but perhaps they weren't so cordial to each other.'

'Why did you find your relationship to Maynard interesting?'

'Because we were so different.'

'What did you like about Maynard?'

'Everything, but of course his extreme cleverness. And his marked kindness to *me*.'

'Did he ever rebuke or scold you?'

'Just for little things.'

'Like what?'

'How can I possibly remember . . . It could have been behaviour at table.'

'Weren't your manners impeccable?'

'I should have hoped so.'

'Perhaps it was for not passing things?'

'Something like that.'

'You hadn't begun your affair with Vanessa then, had you?'

'No, I hardly knew her. She got on well with Maynard, and very well with Lytton.'

'Did Virginia get on well with Lytton?'

'I think so, but less well than Vanessa.'

*   *   *   *   *

Well, it is done. A light tan brushed-cotton suit has been bought for £12, and this is what Duncan will wear on the morning of our departure. I say *morning* because I have mistaken morning for evening and have only just realised it. We are to rise into the skies tomorrow, Sunday, at 9.20 *a.m.* not p.m. This means being at Heathrow at 8.20, which means leaving the house at 7.20 and getting up at about six. It now strikes me as ridiculous that we have arranged a small dinner here tonight. The flat is strewn with our luggage; there will be the washing-up, and what if our guests linger?

Angelica* and Fanny Garnett arrive in good time bringing the dinner they have cooked. I open the front door to them and they stagger up the steps with an enormous quiche Lorraine and a no less behemoth grey mullet in a deep dish, swimming posthumously in aromatic juices and white wine. There is also a salad and an apple turnover. Duncan is supplying the wine, which I picked up in Marylebone High Street earlier. It is something better than the giant bottles of red plonk we usually give ourselves.

Eardley Knollys, too, has arrived, looking as archiepiscopally *Cantuariensis* as ever. It seems this evening that he and Fanny Garnett are to take different views about everything. He counters her Bloomsbury 'What do you mean by that?' with 'I should have thought it is obvious.' They spar through the meal, usually entertainingly but sometimes very near the bone. As for me, I find it a prince of a dinner and can barely keep from making a pig of myself.

* * * * *

'What were the meals like, Duncan, during those week-ends when you, Vanessa and Clive, Lytton and Maynard, used to stay with Ottoline Morrell at Garsington?'

'Well cooked but small. Everything was eaten by the end.'

'How many people usually?'

'Between six and eight, but sometimes there were twenty over the week-end and possibly even sitting down.'

'From Friday evening till Monday morning?'

'Yes . . . Tom Eliot was often there, and Aldous Huxley.'

'Did you like Eliot?'

'Very much. And later when he married I think I was a help to him when his wife began to go mad. He used to ask me round because I got on well with her. Once she left the room unexpectedly and soon there was a particular scent in the air — like a drug — and Tom looked upset and asked me to leave immediately.'

'A sad marriage — he a forced eunuch all those years . . . No wonder he became a master of negation in *The Wasteland*! . . . How did you like Aldous?'

'Quite, though we never felt completely at home with him. We thought he rather abused Ott's hospitality.'

'In what way?'

---

* Duncan's and Vanessa Bell's daughter.

'He did what he liked.'

'Didn't you all?'

'No, we were all agog to behave as was expected of us. Aldous didn't obey the rules of the house . . .'

'Whereas you did?'

'Yes . . . and he'd say derogatory things.'

'Such as?'

'Well, Lytton might remark: "We're having chicken for luncheon," and Aldous would answer: "No, it's the peacock at last" — about which they had been talking expectantly for months—and then add: "You know how old and scraggy that will be." '

'It seems to me that you were all very young and all very hungry.'

'Yes, but the intellectual fare was the thing. It had to sustain us.'

'And was the conversation good?'

'Very.'

'With Ottoline presiding and reigning over it all — "en grande tenue", as William Plomer said later in a marvellous poem?'

'Yes, very much that.'

'And was there mainly one conversation at a time — you know, the way Christabel Aberconway used to do, with everything more or less addressed to the Chair?'

'Yes, Ott wouldn't have countenanced anything else. She got us all going on a subject and kept us there. She had a deep musical voice that sailed over everything . . . I remember once afterwards when we were all going up to bed (Vanessa, Lytton and I), and saying goodnight outside Lytton's bedroom and his exclaiming: "Wasn't it marvellous!" and Vanessa answering: "If you like that sort of thing", and me not being enthusiastic. Lytton was amazed and disappointed.'

'Did Ottoline allow Aldous more liberties than the rest of you?'

'She seemed to . . . Though later she had an affair with Lytton.'

'What? You never told me that!'

'Well, they went off somewhere near Pangbourne together. Lytton was in a great stew because of Henry Lamb.'

'Henry Lamb — the painter?'

'Yes. He was there too, having a real affair with Ottoline — I mean intercourse and everything.'

'But wasn't Lytton's real, wasn't there sex?'

'Yes, but only kissing and hugging . . . You see Ottoline thought she could save Lytton from being a bugger . . . Lytton used to confide in me.'

'Didn't Ottoline's husband mind these goings-on?'

'He made up his mind not to mind.'

*   *   *   *   *

It is not yet midnight and our three guests have considerately gone. I ring up a car hire service called the Brunswick Car Hire Limited (one we have never used before but the only one which answers) and ask: 'Can a car pick us up at 7 a.m.?' They can. But the moment I put the telephone down, a thought occurs to me. 'Why don't we take the car all the way to Heathrow,' I say, 'instead of booking it only to the terminal in Kensington? What a lot of fuss and bother this will avoid.' 'Oh no,' says Duncan, 'that would be far too extravagant.' 'Think of it,' I press, 'only one getting-in-and-out of the taxi with all our bags, and none of the business of waiting around for the bus. Besides, we can have an extra hour in bed.'

While Duncan is still demurring I get the Brunswick Car Hire again and arrange for us to be called at 8 a.m. instead of seven. For £3 they are to drive us all the way to the airport.

September 16th

Things are going with ominous smoothness. Even the wheelchair I asked BEA to have ready at Heathrow is there. A friendly and competent orderly insists on doing the wheeling, though I wanted to do that myself. But it is just as well, because with him wheeling, Duncan sails through the formalities. Instead of having to mount the little bus which takes one to the plane, we are hoisted by lift on to our own truck and do not have to walk up steps into the plane but are deposited at the very door with the cooked lunches. Once in our seats, we give ourselves over to the euphoria-like torpor which, thank heaven, we both succumb to whenever we travel by air. Of course, the bloody marys help. I have brought an outsized flask of them.

'Do you remember our train journey to King's Lynn on the 8th of January 1973 for the opening of your show at the Fermoy Gallery?'

'Indeed I do, Don.'*

'Not as well as I do. I came all the way back from being poet-in-residence in California just to take you.'

'So you say.'

'It was a triumph and a near disaster. You lived up to your honorary DD.'

'Did I?'

'Yes, Doctor of Drink.'

'Tease!'

'No, the truth . . . I see the plane is filling up. Have another bloody mary.'

'Please.'

---

* One of the author's names, and the one by which Duncan Grant always called him.

January 8th 1973   3 Park Square West   3.45 p.m.

D.G., on the threshold of his eighty-ninth year, is dressed in his best suit (one of the C & A successes), wearing a startling tie I have brought back from California and a pink rose in his buttonhole. The bell rings.

'It's the cab at last. I'll take our bags upstairs* and let the taxi-man know we're on our way . . . There's no real hurry, Duncan.'

'Come straight back.'

'No, I'm deserting you.'

On my way back from the front door I hear a falling noise – crumple crumple crumple – my God, Duncan's falling downstairs!

I find him lying at the bottom of the stairs with his feet in the air and a beatific grin on his face. He appears to be unhurt but later in the taxi I am not so sure.

'Duncan, are you all right?'

'Why shouldn't I be . . . I wish you'd tell me where we're going.'

'You know very well: Liverpool Street to catch the 4.36 for King's Lynn.'

'Good gracious! Whatever for?'

'For the opening of your show at Lady Fermoy's Gallery – you know, Mary Berry's mother – a lady-in-waiting to the Queen Mum.'

'I know no such thing.'

I think: 'My God! he's lost his memory. I'm going to arrive in King's Lynn with a nearly-nonagenarian idiot.' The taxi is now in sight of the neo-Gothic and pink orotund glories of St Pancras.

'Duncan, surely you remember the show of recent work Lady Fermoy has arranged with Anthony d'Offay?'

'Very clever of them, no doubt, but nothing to do with me . . . I think we'd better ask the cab to take us to tea and crumpets somewhere.'

'Wouldn't you prefer a nice bloody mary?'

'Ah . . . well . . . perhaps. . .'

'Shall we get into the train first?'

At Liverpool Street Station we walk slowly to the train and mount the first carriage. Duncan, settled in a corner-seat facing the engine, seems content but still in obvious oblivion. I pour out the first bloody marys from our powerful provender (mine are never less than half-and-half, impassioned with a little mustard and given a cheesy tang with a thimbleful of whiskey), and he downs it. 'Another?' 'Yes.' The train gathers speed northwards. Welwyn Garden City has hardly slipped by and Duncan has had three. He is now asleep . . . Please God, let him wake up sane!

At roughly ten to seven and long since dark, the train draws up at King's Lynn

---

* The flat was in the basement.

station. Our having seized the first compartment at Liverpool Street does not now pay off: we are half a mile from the barrier and we walk with baby steps in agonising slowness; but, oh, wonder of wonders! Duncan's memory has returned. He knows the why and the wherefore. And there they are in the distance: Lady Fermoy and her welcoming party.

Almost the first thing that happens in the Gallery — we are given full glasses of claret. Notables throng, the pictures sing, Duncan is surrounded. I think he is being coherent but dare not get too near — though I should, for he has just accepted a second glass.

It is about 8.15. Lady Fermoy has driven us to her lovely house at Uphall, about six miles away, where we are to dine. The other guests are Raymond Leppard, the conductor, and Derry Moore, the son of Joan Moore the concert pianist and Lord Drogheda. Pre-dinner drinks are proffered and before I know it Raymond Leppard has handed Duncan a tumbler of nearly neat gin. Duncan — 'never been known to refuse a drink' — is already well into it. We move to the smaller dining-room and seat ourselves at the elegant round table. The atmosphere is exquisite and *intime* . . . But oh, the soup is still being sipped and it is obvious that Duncan is sodden! His dropped head is only an inch from his plate; the soup is removed; conversation flows on. Raymond Leppard is now telling me that he would give anything to possess a Duncan Grant figure drawing, while the maestro himself — all glass and cutlery put out of reach — quaffs from an imaginary goblet which he raises again and again to his lips. Lady Fermoy, the soul of delicacy, smiles understandingly and observes that tomorrow morning at eleven the Queen Mother is to visit the Gallery to see Duncan's pictures. She turns to me.

'Will he be all right?'

'Oh yes,' I say with misgivings.

The dessert has been served and Duncan is now asleep, with his head tucked into his breast. The dinner concludes with brandy and cigars. Derry Moore and I carry Duncan up to his bedroom. It is agreed that I occupy the other bed.

At about 4 a.m. I wake up and see the bedroom door opened and Duncan heading unsteadily down the passage. I spring out of bed.

'What do you think you're doing?'

'There's a woman with a baby in the bed next to mine,' he says.

'That's me. Come back.'

It must be about 8.30. A maid has come in, drawn the curtains, and brought us breakfast: cereals, buttered toast, bacon and eggs, marmalade and coffee. We sit up in our beds and enjoy it. Duncan, who missed his dinner, eats everything. He seems to be blissfully without hangover — even debonair. Outside, a soft misty morning accentuates our comfort. Our windows look on to lawns, rosebeds and apple trees. I draw a full bath for him and help him into the well-appointed bathroom. Soon he is

14

splashing and wallowing like a grampus. There is a knock at the door and Lady Fermoy's voice, a little anxious, enquires:

'Is he all right?'

'Quite.'

'We must leave for the Gallery at about 10.30,' she says.

The Queen Mother's visit to the Gallery is a success. The legendary naturalness and charm of her presence are real. She comes with two ladies-in-waiting and we have the Gallery to ourselves. Duncan pays his obeisances and accompanies the Queen. She is enthusiastic. She already possesses three 'Duncans' (including the two fine paintings of St Paul's – early and late – hanging in the show) and would like another. She and he walk slowly round the Gallery. Near a certain picture I hear her say:

'That's lovely. Perhaps that's the one I should have.'

'Oh no, Ma'm,' I hear him answer, 'that's a very dull picture. I wouldn't advise it.'

I decide that Duncan must be separated from the Queen and I skilfully insert myself between them. She continues the tour with *me*, Duncan now trailing behind with the ladies-in-waiting. The Queen Mother's alertness and the precision of her comments surprise me. These are no vague eulogisms. She says things like: 'Just look at the way he has painted that studio stove! It ought to be a boring patch of iron-grey, and it isn't. There is so much life in it.'

This encourages me to tell her of my foreword to the show which because of a printers' strike was never printed. In it I explained how Duncan's paintings had educated my own eye and why it is that his work never fails to grow upon the beholder. The Queen asks me to be sure to send her a copy. Then we come to a picture called *Still Life with Matisse*, in which a blue Matisse cut-out figures behind a typical Duncan composition of objects and flowers.

'Oh dear,' she exclaims, 'I should like to buy every painting here. I wish I could afford it.' Then turning to me with her warming smile she adds: 'This one is so lovely I don't think I can resist it.'

Casting a look back at Duncan, luckily out of hearing, I say: 'Your Majesty has chosen well.'

*   *   *   *   *

We are now in the air heading for Istanbul. My general air-travel euphoria with its wide feelings of forgiveness for the world's sins and its pantheistic sense that we are flying through God (all warmed into fuller presence, no doubt, by the bloody marys) receives a jolt. For unaccountably I begin to think of the Turks as the rapists of Lawrence of Arabia. I look at Duncan asleep and shudder. What is it that lurks at the back of my mind? One of the games I play with him in the mornings just before rousing him is the game of lecherous Turk swooping on sleeping Armenian damsel. It is not that I imagine such a barbarity to be funny but that Duncan's reaction to this tease *is*. The 'Turk' leers, ogles and prepares to pounce. The Duncan-damsel with terror in her eyes clutches the bedclothes and pleads. Her cries are so convincing that usually the panting Turk shows mercy, but once in a while his lasciviousness cannot be stayed and in a rude and mighty snatch he exposes her virgin vulnerability to the world.

Now, at the start of our adventure, the unpleasant thought occurs: can this perverted frolic come to roost? One of our friends hearing of our journey said: 'You *are* brave!' I hope he was just thinking that neither of us spoke a word of Turkish. But was it for nothing that one of my grandfathers had actually been Armenian? A fact, incidentally, never overlooked by Duncan in his stock counter-ploy to my ravishing Turk, linking it to the Jewishness of my great-great-grandfather, Ignaz Moscheles – the composer and pianist.

'It's well known,' says Duncan, 'that the Armenian Jew is the lowest you can sink.' To which I have no reply but: 'It's also well known that no Jew can exist in Scotland.'

Not all is right when three and a half hours later we land at Istanbul, 3 p.m. their time. I sense it in the wretched airport, hardly more than a jumble of extended shacks. Duncan's new blue cylindrical canvas bag comes rumbling past on the luggage belt but my false-leather black one does not. The various officials I appeal to return me an empty-eyed robot gaze. No wonder, for they do not understand a word I am saying. Two Americans have also lost their bags and though I have to wait endlessly while each in turn fills out forms, they at least have found the right person to address. Her name is Betty – a brisk young Turk.

In the dingy shambles, it is difficult to find a place where Duncan can sit. He shows signs of tiredness. He is beginning to shuffle. I always have to force myself to remember that he is in his eighty-ninth year, for age has no part in his buoyant and mercurial spirit. 'Duncan, you will never grow old,' Roger Fry once said to him. 'Why not?' 'Because you have a mind.'

It is now 4.30 p.m. Our plane for Antalya does not leave until 10.40 tonight: over six hours to fill in – too much for comfort and not enough to make it worthwhile going into Istanbul encumbered as we are with bag and baskets (for there are no lockers in this miserable airport). We take a taxi to a big new hotel nearby which our tourist agent in South Molton Street recommended. It is the best we can do, but our hearts sink when we see this brash tall box of a building rising up like a Hilton-on-the-Bosporus: the jewel no doubt of an up-and-coming neighbourhood. Compared to it, even suburban Reading seems to me a Mecca of beauty.

'What shall we do, Duncan, for the next six hours in these dismal purlieus?'

'Have a siesta,' he says, 'if we can find a place.'

I settle him on a smart inhuman-looking sofa and go off roaming. At least the sun is stronger here than in Reading, and there are flowers – flowers I have not seen since my days in Mexico and India – canna, hibiscus and bougainvilleas. I walk through the

16

gardens and along the water's edge, managing to be gone for about an hour and a half. When I come back I find Duncan off his sofa and sipping raki: a drink that turns white when you pour water into it.

'That was clever of you,' I say. 'How did you make anyone understand?'

'Need finds its own ways.'

I congratulate him and join him by swigging the last of our bloody marys. Then, arm in arm, we sway down the grand staircase into dinner. Raki, I see, acts with devastating swiftness on an empty stomach. The orchestra is playing the favourite of its three tunes: 'Scarborough Fair'. The other two prove to be 'Santa Lucia' and 'La Donna e Mobile'. We seat ourselves among a swirl of waiters and order a bottle of wine: our first bottle of Turkish, and we are curious. It turns out to be undistinguished, raw but honest. The rest of the meal is indifferent. Duncan finds his kebab tough and gives half of it to me. There is cucumber-tomato-feta salad, which we shall soon discover is as inevitable in Turkey as in Greece. We end the meal with ice-cream and coffee. The bill comes to 216 Turkish lira — about £6. Which seems to me a bit steep, considering this is not Paris or London.

11.45 p.m. We are at the airport again, in the dingiest of waiting-rooms, waiting and waiting with the milling passengers for the plane to Antalya to let us board. There it is, the plane, sitting on the ground in full view — and has been for the last two hours — but nothing happens. Then, in my wanderings, I come upon a disturbing scene and the cause of our delay: an old Turk is having a stroke. He is stretched out on the only bench there is, his cheeks sucked in and his face the colour of Camembert. Distraught relatives do their best: prop him up, lay him down, fan him, whisper. I pray that Duncan has not noticed him, but Duncan has and his perspicacity cuts through the nasty thought nagging my mind:

'Good job it's not me,' he exclaims, puffing on his Marmora (a small cigar).

'Try another,' I say. 'That one's as solid as mahogany . . . Mine was too. They simply won't draw.'

He takes another Marmora from the flashy cellophane packet I hand him and puffs furiously. We laugh. It is like trying to draw air through a cylinder of wood.

Still no move to board the plane, though people queue and then unqueue again. I walk Duncan slowly to where the old man is out of sight . . . What I do not know is that this is the last holiday I shall have with Duncan walking.

12.15 a.m. Our ragged file still waiting to board the Turk Hava Yollari plane is at last allowed to mount. We take our seats, Duncan collapses into a deep sleep, nothing happens. Behind me I hear heaving, murmuring, arranging. I know it! When shall I dare look round? Fate is so insultingly predictable. Of all the fifty places in the plane to choose from, where should they put the dying old man but right behind Duncan. Yes, he is there; I look. They have hauled him aboard. But things are not going right. Air hostesses with naively sophisticated coiffures beginning to crumble after several days of late nights, bounce down the aisle with worried faces. It is hot. The air hostesses are bedewed with a sort of country-girl pink sweat. Strong young men in braid issue from the sacrosanctum of the pilot's lodge. I see what looks like an oxygen cylinder being bundled aft. I dare to look round again. It gives me a pang. The old man is still breathing but only just. There is little conversation in our air-lozenge. People are too tired. Or do they know what is going on? . . . Ah, but some kind of order has at last been given. It is nearly one o'clock in the morning and suddenly the engines roar. We slide into the air. I look round for the last time. The old Turk is dead. A distressed matron stands behind him swaddling his head in a scarf. Duncan sleeps.

*   *   *   *   *

The idea has just occurred to me that I ought to keep a journal on this trip: one that will give an account of our days without too deeply involving *me*. I mean, I want it to be mainly about Duncan and rarely go into my own thoughts and feelings. Will such a journal seem incomplete and perhaps obsessive? If so, *tant pis*. I am not prepared at this still 'ungelled' stage of my life to take on my autobiography. Anything to do with Duncan, yes. That is different.

At the moment, as we speed through the night skies towards Antalya, I am for some reason pondering upon Duncan's relations with Vanessa – whom I still often think of. To me she was a quietly powerful and awesome figure. I suppose it was natural for her to regard me with suspicion and a certain amount of resentment. Now, I think it a pity that I never took the trouble to get close to her. I suppose I could have taken the trouble, but she seemed so remote. Compared to Duncan she was almost venerable – or at least she made me feel like a teenager – and she was to be revered like a grand-mother; whereas Duncan was both my father and my brother. Once when he was worrying about her feelings – in the days when he used to come up to London in the middle of the week to draw and paint me – I remember his saying:

'Some people make things so difficult . . . Vanessa has never really got over Julian's death. She has never really become herself again.'

'Was he an attractive character?' I asked.

'Immensely attractive . . . He was killed in Spain: bombed driving a bus in an ambulance brigade.'

'Was he the eldest of Vanessa's three children?'

'Yes. The last was Angelica.'

'Your daughter?'

'Yes, but that wasn't made common knowledge.'

'When did you first make love to Vanessa?'

'It was at a house-party. I think at the Sitwells'.'

18

'Didn't Clive mind?'

'No, he'd long been having his own mistresses. In fact, Clive burst into the room while we were at it and went straight through to the next room.'

'Wasn't that something of a shock to you?'

'It was.'

'Did he say anything?'

'Yes, he said: "Oh, don't stop. Please go on." '

'And did you?'

'Of course.'

During this conversation I realised that these were things Duncan had never revealed to anybody before, and I felt a little mean as I pressed on.

'Was Angelica conceived on purpose or did you simply wait till it happened?'

'It was all very much on the cards from the start.'

'And were you and Vanessa pleased when it happened?'

'Very.'

'Not at all apprehensive?'

'Not in the least.'

As I write these words I realise how difficult it is for anyone nowadays to have an idea of the unconventionality and the courage of such behaviour at that time: as unconventional and courageous as Duncan's and Bunny Garnett's being conscientious objectors during the First World War; as unconventional and courageous as Clive Bell who, coming from the hunting, shooting, fishing squirearchy as he did, nevertheless wrote a strongly argued pamphlet *against* England's headlong euphoric plunge into spurious 'glory' in 1914 . . . Our conversation continued.

'How long had the affair been going on before Vanessa became pregnant?'

'About a year.'

'Why didn't Vanessa have more children by you after Angelica?'

'I think she wanted to but I stopped sleeping with her after Angelica . . . I mean, even before Angelica was born.'

'Why was that?'

'I made up my mind it was better . . . I remember the morning I told her. It was a day I had to go up to London to see my dealer, I think it was Freddie Mayor, and the first thing he said to me was: "What's happened? You look so at peace and relieved." '

'And were you?'

'Yes. It had become a great ordeal to me.'

'It was costing you too much?'

'Yes . . . You must remember that all this time David Garnett and I were living in the same house, sharing the same bed.'

'What! Were you and David lovers?'

'Yes.'

'I thought David was the great heterosexual of all time — forever in love with a woman?'

'He was, but he could still make love to me.'

'Which did he prefer — boys or girls?'

'Girls.'

'Then why wasn't *he* having an affair with Vanessa?'

'Vanessa wouldn't have anything to do with him; though they were apparently on good terms.'

'Vanessa didn't really like him?'

'I think that's true.'

'You must have been in a difficult position.'

'I was: torn in different directions.'

'Your prowess must have been terrific — required no doubt to satisfy both David and Vanessa the same night?'

'Yes, I suppose it was. But I was exhausted, because I was also working all day on the farm.'

'You enjoyed the one and not the other?'

'No, I enjoyed both . . . I never tired physically of Vanessa. It was more subtle than that, psychological. Perhaps spiritually more was being asked of me than I could give.'

'Wasn't it rather hard on Vanessa that her love-life should come to an end so early? Didn't she mind?'

'She did mind, but after all she could have had other lovers. And she'd had Roger before.'

'Did she desert Roger for you?'

'I suppose so.'

'But Roger was much older than you.'

'Yes, almost another generation — like a kind of uncle.'

'And wasn't Roger upset being left? By now his wife was tucked away in an asylum.'

'He must have been upset but he never showed any animosity towards me.'

By this time I thought that I had intruded my questions far enough, but Duncan suddenly said: 'I remember coming back from London after I had been away longer than I expected and Bunny making a confession to me. He confessed that he had tried to rape Vanessa.'

'What?' I said. 'And did she tell you too?'

'She may have just told me, but not in any recriminating way — just as something that was to be expected.'

'Was there ever tension in the air at Charleston about these things?'

'No.'

'And was Clive there too?'

'A lot of the time . . . Mary Hutchinson was his mistress then but she and Nessa weren't really sympathetic to each other and she never stayed very long.'

'Duncan, once long ago you said to me that Vanessa was in love with you and you were not in love with her and had never hidden the fact from her.'

'That is so, though of course I loved her. And she remained in love with me till the last day of her life.'

'How did she die?'

'She had pleurisy and then pleurisy again – a double pleurisy.'

I told Duncan that I had recently come across two drawings he had done of Vanessa on her deathbed – or perhaps just after she had died. 'Do you remember doing them?' I asked.

'Yes. One was done just before she died and one just after. I thought she might be dying but I was by no means sure. The doctor never told me . . . Quentin was there and at one point he said to me: "Tell her that you love her." I did. That was just before the end.'

September 17th

We have been in the air about half an hour. In an aisle seat immediately across from me sits a young man in mufti. I say 'mufti' because he is obviously military: the quality of his brown boots and blue-grey trousers tells me he is American military. He keeps glancing towards Duncan and me, sensing no doubt that we are not Turkish either. The look on his face is both of excitement and apprehension. We do not, however, begin a conversation. I fall asleep.

The loudspeaker is now crackling, the no-smoking sign is flickering: we are about to touch down. I fasten my seat-belt. Duncan's has never been unfastened. We land.

In the neat, pleasantly designed airport of Antalya I direct Duncan slowly to a seat and am wondering what is the next move when the young American comes up and says with a quiver in his voice:

'I sure as hell hope the Navy is here.'

'What Navy?' I ask.

'Why, the American, the US Third Fleet . . . I got a telegram two days ago in San Diego. "Report to naval attaché 3rd Fleet Antalya September 18th," it said . . . I sure hope this is Antalya.'

'I expect so,' I said, 'but today is barely the *17th*.'

'Maybe, but I was scared of missing the Fleet.'

He is about six foot, in his middle twenties, attractively and cleanly built: more intelligent in appearance than the 'all-American boy' but with the same well-scrubbed look and very much the young American officer as I remember him during the war.

He tells me that this is the first time he has left his native United States.

'If the American Fleet is in Antalya,' I reassure him, 'you won't miss it.'

He goes off to speak to an official, not yet realising that his English will not get him far. Duncan and I have by now found and put ourselves into a taxi. The American catches up with us – a lost look on his face – and evidently wants to come too. I have my misgivings but the taxi-driver bundles him in. My instinct tells me that our sharp screwed-up little Turk is going to take us for a ride in more ways than one.

The young man sinks back in his seat with a sigh and holds out his hand to each of us in turn. 'Joe Warren,' he says: 'glad to know you.' We reciprocate and identify ourselves. But where are we going? In South Molton Street I had been given the names of three hotels: the Grand Hotel Buyouk, the Perge and the Darya. We speed through the dark countryside, the time being about one in the morning. I am worried about Duncan. I doubt if he can take much more.

'Ask the driver if he has seen the Fleet,' says the American. I do, in French, but he knows nothing of any fleet. Joe Warren now tries to spell out his anguish in signs. The driver merely shrugs his shoulders and continues.

At the Grand Hotel Buyouk they care not a fig for us. Have we reservations? No. 'In South Molton Street I was told it wouldn't be necessary.' 'Then we can do nothing.' 'But can you suggest anywhere?' 'No, we cannot.' . . . Back into the taxi-cab, where I find Joe Warren asking for the harbour and pleading with the man to locate the Fleet.

'The Fleet can wait till the morning,' I say. 'Let's find a place to sleep.'

We urge the driver on to the Darya on the west side of Antalya. There a party is going on, half in the hotel and half on the beach. A sullen youth tells me in French that the hotel and motel are both full. 'Will you do me the favour of telephoning the Hotel Perge?' Gracelessly, he does. No room there either. A wave of fear sweeps over me. Will Duncan and I actually lie down in the street? I turn to the taxi-driver:

'Do you know a place?'

'Oh yes . . . another fifty to take you there.'

'But that's twice what you asked to bring us all the way from the airport.'

'Lira or dollars?' chips in the American.

Foolish, foolish boy! The man's covetous little eyes twinkle.

'You have dollars?'

'You agreed to lira,' I put in quickly.

Too late. The man is now fixed on dollars. He wants ten dollars from Duncan and me and five from Joe Warren. Fifteen dollars comes to about £6 which is 210 Turkish lira: over four times what we had agreed, and that was already outrageous. But we have no choice.

Outside the tawdry entrance of the 'hotel' he takes us to at two o'clock in the morning, with Duncan hardly able to stand and a vulturine cluster of youths watching us, it is not the time, I decide, to haggle with a dark-eyed Turk in a murky street. So, I pay off the taxi-man and the three of us ascend two flights of stone stairs to our single room: for yes, Duncan, the young American and I are to be closeted together.

The heat and the lack of air in the tiny bedroom are excessive. I prise open a small window; the other window is stuck. Duncan, stripped to his underpants, collapses on the bed and is already asleep. I cover him with a sheet. Joe Warren, after much fussing with the lock, also lies down. We talk from our respective beds.

'One thing I sure must do,' he says with a wry smile, 'is take a photograph of this dump. None of my friends back home will believe I stayed in an outfit like this.'

It is a hellish night. Our hovel turns out to be in the middle of Antalya's Oxford Street. Lorries, with all the impetus of leviathans, lurch through my dreams. Motor bicycles start, splutter and honk. When the man-made noises at last abate, innumerable cocks of innumerable pullet harems cock-a-doodle-doo false dawns.

To be up at eight, tired though we are, is a relief. Joe Warren and I investigate the amenities. The loo is a smelly cubicle with a foot platform and a hole; it abuts the precincts of a seedy drawing-room full of a vaguely Victorian clutter: oleographs of bewhiskered grandfathers, a table with lace doilies, a print of Highland cattle. I feel sure that a madame will soon be presiding in the umbra of this over-stuffed, horse-haired gloom, and I wonder how I can then issue from the bedroom carrying the one beautiful object in the place – a silver urn with a narrow decanter neck once holding bedside drinking-water but now that which Duncan has so copiously filled it with during the night. Luckily, nobody comes before I perform this work of supererogation and I pour his cornucopia on to a row of plants on the outside window sill – hoping it will be a tonic for them. I am even noble enough to rinse out the decanter several times.

Joe Warren is dressed first, raring to search for the Fleet. My concern is to find a proper hotel, then trace my missing bag. The loss of my luggage has wrecked our plans and halted us in Antalya when we wanted to proceed to Side. How can we proceed when I have no clothes? It has also robbed me of the exhilaration I should feel on my first morning in a foreign town. The noise, colour, odours, the warm dusty diaphanous vision of minarets and distant mountains should fill me with elation and an exact response to each. Instead, everything is felt through a blur of disquiet. My lack of zest would better fit Camden Town. Betty, the BEA Turkish girl in Istanbul, told me that my chances of getting the bag back would be greater if I stayed in Istanbul. She could guarantee no success if I tried to negotiate from Antalya. From the village of Side, of course, there would be no chance at all. So, here we are stuck and breakfastless.

My three main problems are these: where to settle Duncan while I hunt for a hotel? Where to find someone who speaks English? And where to telephone Istanbul? I discover that the greatest of these is the last. To telephone Istanbul one must book a call. This might take several hours. The morning staff at the Grand Hotel Buyouk are much nicer than the lot I tried to parley with a few hours before. They still have no room for us but at least they are ready to let Duncan sit on the terrace in the shade of the cypress trees. There I settle him with a cup of coffee and his sketchbook, then I embark on the task of making contact with BEA Betty in Istanbul. I book an emergency call: expensive but supposedly swifter. Joe Warren is at my heels. He has made no progress in finding the Fleet. Will I go with him to the chief of police and ask if he can throw any light on its whereabouts?

'Joe,' I say, 'it isn't necessary. Someone there is sure to speak French or English. You don't need *me*.'

'But I don't know a word of French,' he says.

'All the same, I'm certain you'll manage,' I counter.

The look of dejection on his face makes me add: 'If you don't find the Fleet, I promise at least to help you find a place to stay the night.'

I leave him looking like a small boy lost at the zoo. Perhaps I have been too impatient with him, but the dusty, crowded, noisy town — its beauty beginning to be smeared with the processes of industrial grime — and the worry of my missing luggage, make me not at my best. Besides, it is already hot. The new, flared, black trousers I bought two days ago at Take Six in Oxford Street have no pockets. Why had I not noticed? Oh curse their narcissistic hugging of form! An old sack would be better here. I must wear or carry my jacket everywhere, its every orifice bulging with passports, documents, travellers cheques, purse. Moreover, my feet are stiflingly shod in socks and boots. I had taken it for granted that the one thing one could be sure of finding in Turkey were sandals. Not a bit of it. The Turks seem not so much as to have a word for them.

Meanwhile, I have been hanging around for two hours waiting for my call to Istanbul, dismally beginning to recall some of the important items the lost bag contained: tape-recorder, address book, correspondence, clothes for the next three weeks and, most doomed of all, one hundred pounds in notes. The bag is not locked; it has no key and in any case must be opened by the Turkish customs at Istanbul.

I go back to Duncan on the terrace, relieved to see that though he shows signs of yesterday's exertions he seems oblivious to the problems of life and has completed a charming sketch in charcoal of the red brick minaret we can see through the pine trees. He is already sipping a raki.

Strolling through the hotel gardens overlooking the pretty harbour of Antalya, I suddenly hear Joe Warren's voice: 'Paul, Paul, Istanbul is on the line.' Though I bound over flowerbeds of drying zinnias and dust-laden marigolds, it is not fast enough. Istanbul is off the line. Blast blast blast! . . . 'Joe, did they throw *any* light on my luggage?'

'They said they knew nothing of a black bag and nothing of a BEA Betty'.

I wander into the street with the American and towards the offices of Turk Hava Yollari, the Turkish airlines. Although I have already been there once this morning to describe my loss, I decide to recite my litany again. This time a pretty girl behind the counter not only speaks English but seems concerned. Meanwhile, Joe Warren discovers a teletape machine in an adjoining office.

'Get her to send a detailed description of your bag to Istanbul,' he says. This strikes me as a bright suggestion and it is followed. All I can do now is hope and wait. As we walk back to the Hotel Buyouk I ask him: 'How have you been getting on with the Fleet?'

'Bad. Nobody knows a thing about the goddam Fleet.'

'Why not try the harbour master?'

'Say, that's an idea. Will you come too?'

'Y-yes . . . but first let's see what Duncan's up to, then go and have a first-class lunch.'

I had asked the pretty girl who sent the teletape if she knew of an unpretentious restaurant where we could eat Turkish food. 'Yes, the Sherik,' she said, and told us how to get there. It is off the market; a part of the world I have already explored in my search for sandals. The three of us – Duncan still very slow – get into a taxi.

During the ride I notice Joe Warren fumbling with his wallet. Then he blurts out: 'If the Fleet doesn't arrive I'm sure in trouble.' Sheepishly he tells us that he has come all this way with enough money for only about two days.

'You see, the Navy has everything,' he puts in wistfully. 'It's a damned floating universe.'

To me it seems both absurd and touching that this young man should have put so much faith in the Navy that a single telegram could have him prancing over the ocean to the motherly bosom of the Fleet without a thought of betrayal. No wonder the sweep of blue bay and the lonely backdrop of the Taurus Mountains unbroken by the silhouette of a single American warship fill him with despair.

When Joe Warren is off looking for the bathroom at the Sherik, I remark to Duncan: 'The fleshpots of the Fleet were to have solved everything for him.'

'So it seems, and now I dare say we shall have to lend him money.'

'He feels safe with us, even when it comes to eating.'

'Especially when it comes to eating,' Duncan adds.

Joe Warren comes back gleaming with cleanliness and glowing with praise. 'Why, you couldn't find a cleaner kitchen even back home!' Certainly, the floor is freshly swept, the long freezer flawlessly white, and the table-cloths spotless. We notice, however, that he does not trust the hygiene of the glasses and drinks his beer straight from the bottle. What interests Duncan and me quite as much as the sanitary brightness of the place is the number of obviously contented eaters. It is a spacious dining-room and every table is taken.

There are no menus. One orders whatever is going or what one inspects in kitchen and freezer. I convey to the waiter that we want boiled lamb and a dish called *cacik* – described in the guidebook as 'small cubes of cucumber and crushed garlic blended with yoghourt and a few drops of olive oil'. The boiled lamb is a concession to Joe Warren who says: 'Wouldn't that be safest?' I see him now playing with the *cacik* as if it were a dish of scorpions – having first assiduously wiped his plate with the napkin and then his knife and fork – but he *is* eating the *cacik* and with growing relish. To Duncan and me it seems nothing less than a creamy bowl of chilled ambrosia.

Then says the young American, downing a second beer from the bottle as Duncan and I start on a forbidden melon, 'My job in the States has to do with gastronomic hygiene.' We look at each other thinking: 'So that's it!'

The Sherik is the kind of restaurant I long to find in any foreign town: a place the small businessman frequents, bringing sometimes his wife or mistress and at week-ends his family. It is indigenous, it is unpretentious. The food is excellent and cheap, the waiting swift and honest, and no one expects a big tip. I have found such a place in the heart of Mexico City, and one such in Athens. No doubt here and there in London – perhaps off the Strand or in the City – it still exists. In Antalya it is the Sherik. The fine luncheon we have been served cost a quarter of our travesty of a dinner in Istanbul.

It is two o'clock. Duncan, Joe Warren and I all feel happier. We are in a taxi taking us to the Pension Villa Park – for, yes, my one success of the morning was to discover a place to sleep.

'You won't believe it,' I say, 'it has trees all around and it's actually quiet. The only drawback is a circular staircase Duncan'll have to climb. But it's a big airy room with wide windows.'

'Are we all going to be in one room?' asks Joe.

'Yes. It was that or nothing.'

'Suits me,' he says. 'I couldn't afford a single room.'

Twenty minutes later, we are ensconced. I have the middle bed, Duncan's is near the door, Joe Warren has chosen the one nearest the windows.

'Back home we'd have air-conditioning,' he says.

'I know,' I reply. 'I've caught many a cold because of it. And you even have it in your cars . . . No chance of the hood down on a hot evening and the lovely warm air wafting past.'

The clean lines of his regular features pucker. Was I misguided or simply perverse? How unevolved could these damned English be! He swallows and says: 'Down in San Diego we have *some* heat. Even you would get tired of it.'

By this time Duncan is all tucked up and has begun his siesta. I have drawn the curtains (regretfully cutting out the strong sun) and am tossing off my hot boots and hateful trousers when our young companion plunges past me towards the door.

'A helicopter,' he shouts. 'I sure know that throb. It's a truly American 'copter. The Fleet's on its way.'

I hear him fling himself down the circular staircase. It is the last thing I hear.

Waking about five, after the densest of siestas, I feel compelled to go into the sun – which has by no means lost all its vigour. I have my shirt off even before leaving the villa compound. In these three weeks – even in September – I mean to get brown.

A fine Roman ruin presides over the cliff, where a rocky path leads down to the sea. I have not plunged into the Mediterranean since my days in Corfu eleven years ago and never have I plunged into the Aegean. I do so now and swim deliciously far enough out to see the whole of the beautiful bay.

On my way back I take a closer look at the ruin on the cliff and find it is what the guidebook calls the Tower of Hidirlik, built during the second century at the southern extremity of the old wall. Its base is square but its second storey round. Perhaps it was a lighthouse once. While admiring this building, I see a youth in a yellow shirt making signs at me and hissing. He approaches over the broken ground and furiously indicates that he has something to impart. Summoning me into the deep shade of fig and cane, he runs through a breathlessly inventive repertoire of gestures: 'What is your need? Boy or girl? Back or front? Oral or anal?'

I let him run out of signs, then primly indicate: 'Not today, thank you. If I do require anything it'll be a woman.'

'Yes yes, I have good woman,' he counters: 'Only one hundred lira.'

As I walk away prices topple. By the time I reach the villa compound 'good woman' has dropped to eight.

To my surprise I find Duncan sitting amid the debris of the hotel yard. Someone has brought him a chair from the house and there he is sketching among the empty cigarette cartons, random caster-oil plants and dried-up grasses. I tell him about the boy in the yellow shirt.

'Was he good-looking?'

'No, hideous,' I say. 'His teeth stuck out and he had a mean face.'

'Perhaps you'll have a chance to follow it up.'

'I expect I shall. He probably lurks there every evening.'

September 18th

We are woken this morning (that is, Duncan and I; there is no stir from the American) by a robust knock and there is the lad who runs this place – he is only about sixteen – standing with a breakfast tray of fresh bread, feta and jam, and little glasses of hot tea.

Joe Warren is stretched naked and motionless, not even covered by a sheet. I wonder he does not feel the chill of the morning air blowing in through the open windows.

'I could use him as a model,' Duncan remarks. 'He has a pretty body.'

'Yes, I saw that yesterday,' I say, 'in our Black Hole of Calcutta.'

The two of us sit down on the balcony, where I have carried the tray. There are pine trees in the Park and creepers on the balustrade. I am luxuriating already in the sun. It is while I pour a second glass of tea that Joe Warren bursts on to the terrace in his underpants and gazes piercingly at the sky, the sea, the horizon; which are all exactly as they were yesterday: a blue sky, a blue bay, and a horizon unmarred by the gunmetal presence of a single warship. The young man sniffs and cocks his ear.

'The Fleet's just round the corner. I'm damned sure of it,' he says. 'I've got to spruce myself up.'

He hurries back into the bedroom but immediately doubles out again.

'Say, d'you guys have a razor? My shaver won't fit the goddam Turkish slots.'

'Don't worry. Duncan'll lend you his.'

I feel proud of myself. I bought Duncan a new electric razor in Selfridges and even had the foresight to provide it with a spare plug guaranteed to fit the slots of Turkey.

Joe Warren emerges in a few minutes looking more scrubbed than ever.

'Have some breakfast,' I say.

'Couldn't possibly. I'm far too excited.'

He has time, however, to notice Duncan, and smiles. Duncan sitting in his drawers with a big straw hat on his head is an arresting and endearing sight. While we are still enjoying our bread and jam and hot tea (without milk), a taxi-cab and then another draw up in the street below and out of them come forth, with a certain amount of heaving and clatter, a group of what look like American businessmen: one of them dressed up as an admiral all in white. It seems unbelievable but this must be the torpedo-head of the American Navy. They are all past middle age. By what quirk of fate have these superannuated sailor-playing tycoons elected the Pension Villa Park to stay in? I shout to Joe Warren: 'The Fleet's arrived.' We hear him flying down the circular staircase almost without touching it. Duncan and I lean over the balcony and watch.

The first words of the 'admiral' to our young friend (who looks like a schoolboy among the group) are: 'What the hell are you doing here? Why the blankety-blank didn't you get in touch with me?'

'I wasn't sure where, sir . . .' began Joe Warren.

'Hell, I'm your Naval Attaché . . . How long have you been here?'

'I came on the night of the 16th, sir.'

'Good God! You were told to report on the 18th.'

I do not catch Joe Warren's reply but he looks chastened. The touching thing about the whole situation is that the young man is – as he told us yesterday – on the Naval

Reserve, has not been to sea for some years and has pulled a great many strings back in Washington and San Diego to land himself a fortnight's jamboree with the Fleet on the Aegean. The businessmen of a certain age who have bundled out of the cabs are undoubtedly his fellow reservists. Here they all are, and by the supremest irony the Naval Attaché has arranged for them to stay in our *pension* until the US Navy can gather them, safe and sound, into her hot-dogged, wonder-breaded, hamburger-bound, aseptic lap.

When Joe Warren comes upstairs to collect his things and say goodbye, I ask wickedly: 'Who is the admiral?'

'He's not an admiral,' Joe answers a little tetchily, 'only an attaché.'

'Will you have dinner with us tonight?' I say. 'Duncan and I are going to eat at the Hotel Perge – you can almost see it from here just across the Park.'

'Thanks, Paul, but I've got to keep myself free . . . Though I may well be there with some of the Navy.'

Duncan and I are glad not to have seen the last of our American, for whom we have begun to feel some responsibility. When I look out over the terrace again, I see that the bay swarms with huge blue-grey shapes etched against the Lycian Mountains. The sun pours down but I have nothing clean or cool to wear.

'Duncan, I'm going into town to see if there's any news of my bag. Shall I set you up to sketch in the Park?'

He gives me his pet-spaniel why-do-you-desert-me look and says: 'Suppose you never come back?'

'That's exactly what I am contemplating . . . Come on now. We'll take your little folding seat along.'

'No. It topples over and pitches me to the ground.'

'That's because you don't sit on it properly.'

'I don't care. I'd rather sit on a stone.'

I am sorry that the small folding stool I scoured London to find on our last day is to prove useless. I walk with Duncan into the Park carrying his sketchbook and pastels and settle him on a bench facing the sea and the mountains. Then I take a taxi to the Grand Hotel Buyouk, where I have made friends with the proprietor: a short man with a grizzled Roman emperor head who speaks English. Yesterday he wrote out sentences for me in Turkish: 'Has my bag come yet?' . . . 'I can't wait any longer.' . . . 'I am returning in half an hour.' He also wrote out the Turkish for sandals and pipe tobacco: both unobtainable.

I hardly expect news of my luggage at the Buyouk, and there is none, but when I call at the offices of Turk Hava Yollari the pretty girl who sent the teletape message yesterday is beaming. She leads me into a tiny room. There, slumped in a corner among dusty parcels, is my bag, hardly recognisable: scratched, grime-covered, held together by an ancient many-knotted cord and looking as though the Turkish army has kicked it around Asia Minor, but still, unmistakably, my bag. The central zip is ripped off as if a Neanderthal man has been tearing into the hide of a stag. My joy is great. Now, to find out how much has been filched. I carry the bag back to the Grand Hotel Buyouk, seek a corner and nervously wrestle with the knots that bind it. I do not expect my tape-recorder to be there. But it *is*. More unbelievable, so are the £100 in notes. Only one thing mars my happiness: the bag is useless. I go to the Roman emperor and ask him: 'Can I find anyone in Antalya to mend a zip?'

He lifts a pair of magnificent white eyebrows: 'In Antalya – not likely.'

'Will you write out a few more Turkish sentences for me?'

'Of course!'

Under my English, in flowing Arabic hieroglyphics, he writes the Turkish for: 'Can you mend a zip? . . . Do you have a strap? . . . I shall be back in an hour.' These shibboleths I tuck away for future use. Now there is something else to be done, for I have just found out that the Hotel Perge at last has a room for us. A little selfishly I decide to move Duncan and me into it. There is nowhere to swim or lie in the sun at the Villa Park, whereas the Perge has its own terraces hanging over the ocean and, most irresistible of all, a paradisal rock pool in the sea. I tell myself that there are advantages to Duncan too: a restaurant, easy chairs, and painterly vistas through the gardens of the Park and over the ever-changing Aegean. Unfortunately, there are also three flights of stairs to our room.

I hurry back to the still sketching Duncan and tell him of our prospective move.

'Do whatever you like,' he says, 'but don't desert *me*. You've been away far too long.'

'But, Duncan, rejoice with me, for the bag that was lost is found.'

'I'm glad to hear it.'

There is no time to brood on this seeming lack of enthusiasm – which I put down to the heat – for we must be out of our room by one and I must organise our exodus from the Pension Villa Park.

'You don't have to do a thing, Duncan. I'll do it all. Give me half an hour. Just time for you to finish your sketch.'

'Half an hour,' he repeats with a black look, and I am off.

Although the Perge is only a stone's throw from our room at the Pension Villa Park, rather than go back and forth carrying bags – the disembowelled carcass of my bag is uncarryable anyway – I hail a taxi and do it all in one swoop. I hurry. The sea beckons. Once in the privacy of the new room, I rip off my sweaty clothes, get into shorts and race down the excitingly steep, almost perpendicular, steps of the hotel to the rock pool. A moment or two more and I have plunged into the Aegean. That first swim of the day and that first lying naked in the sun afterwards – though done with a certain pressure of guilt for having left Duncan – give me my first spasm of joy.

It is well after one o'clock when I rejoin the lonely painter in the Park.

'Deserted again!' are his first words to me.

'Terribly sorry but I couldn't resist a swim . . . Anyway, it gave you lots of time to finish. I like what you've done.' (It is a delicate little sketch in pastel of the Taurus Mountains.)

'It's no use your flattering me. You're in disgrace.'

I see that he is very tired.

'Duncan, are you hungry?'

'Naturally, after all this time.'

'Well, instead of walking to the new hotel – though it's just behind those trees there – why don't we have an alfresco luncheon in these gardens?'

'But do we have anything to eat?'

'Yes, we've got bread, olives and feta cheese – all saved from breakfast. And we can probably get beer from that kiosk over there.'

He agrees that it is a beautiful spot to have lunch, 'and so cool in the shade . . . How amazing of the Turks to grow all these flowers!'

I fetch our provender on the double and we sit down to eat on a bench.

*   *   *   *   *

'Duncan, do you remember that day we once spent on the river at Streatley-on-Thames?'

'Indeed I do. You were a mere stripling.'

'Well, I seemed very young . . . We lolled about in a sort of flat-bottomed boat. It was one of those days in high summer when the Thames valley is hotter than the Mediterranean.'

'I remember encouraging you to garland yourself in water-lilies, Don, and I took photographs.'

'And you drew. But mainly we drifted around in a lovely backwater of willows and weeds . . . In the evening we went back to London.'

'By train?'

'By train . . . Streatley must have been full of memories for you anyway. Didn't you and your parents live there for a short time?'

'For about a year, in a house at the top of the hill lent to us by Uncle Harcourt.'

'What, not the same Harcourt that did all those little sketches of India that are lying about Charleston?'

'Yes. He was married to Aunt Georgie, one of my mother's aunts, who was rather ugly but very lovable. Uncle Harcourt used to take me sketching with him in the punt before breakfast. I must have been about seventeen. It was 1902.'

'I seem to remember your telling me you had some slight illness then and were examined by the local doctor.'

'Yes.'

31

'And what happened?'

'He said there was something obviously wrong with my heart, so my parents thought that perhaps I'd better be taken to a specialist in London.'

'And?'

'There's nothing more to be said . . . Unless I go on.'

'Of course you must go on. What happened when the specialist examined you?'

'He told my father that he didn't think there was anything wrong with my heart. "He's got a muscle that squeaks sometimes when the heart touches it," he said. "It's not in the least serious and you needn't worry any more about it." However, my parents thought it might be a good thing for me to have a holiday in the South of France, because it was midwinter and my Aunt Elinor had a villa there.'

'Who was this Aunt Elinor?'

'Aunt Elinor Colville, my father's sister: a gifted and distinguished lady. She was a friend of Alma Tadema – a bad painter who was all the rage and never painted a picture under £5000.'

'Even then?'

'Even then . . . and she possessed an Alma Tadema . . . Anyway, she asked me to her house in Menton for as long as I liked. And on a cold winter's day – it was January – I left for Menton and stayed the night in Paris on the way'.

'Was that your first visit to Paris?'

'I think it was. I don't think I was ever there before, and I was fascinated by walking about and especially by the little shops in the Palais Royal. There was one shop there given over to licentious literature in the most blatant way. It had rows of paperbacks with English titles. One of them took my fancy: it was called *How We Lost Our Virginity*.'

'About a group of young ladies who . . .?

'Yes, a group of young ladies who described in detail how they lost their maidenheads. I bought it and it amused me during my journey down in the train next day. After that I forgot about it and put it in a drawer with my clothes.'

'Was your aunt's house pretty?'

'Well, I remember arriving there on a January afternoon in blazing sun, delighted to find the roses out in her garden and flowering trees all around. It was a revelation.'

'You said you put *How We Lost Our Virginity* with your clothes. You mean you hid it *under* your clothes?'

'Well, yes, I did: under my shirts and handkerchiefs . . . not because I felt the least bit ashamed about it but just to be on the safe side. I thought no more about it until that terrible man, Harris the butler, who was an unpleasant character . . .'

'You didn't like him from the start, did you?'

'I never liked him. He wasn't sympathetic to me a bit. And he purported to be horrified . . .'

32

'He found it, did he?'

'He found it. By this time it was several weeks after my arrival because Uncle Trevor wasn't there when I got there, but hardly had he stepped into the house when Harris told him all about how he had found *How We Lost Our Virginity* tucked away in my drawer. I dare say he even showed it to him. Uncle Trevor was horrified. He told me he must go to Nice to ask a doctor's advice. What sort of effect might it have on me and so on? The doctor, who I think must have been an extraordinarily stupid man, said: "Oh yes, this sort of thing is the cause of many people's madness. I think your nephew will probably go off his head if he's not careful." So that upset Uncle Trevor even more and he came back and said — though he didn't tell me — that I had done the most awful thing. Eda the maid, who'd been devoted to me until then, turned against me. She was a Prussian of the most vindictive nature and gave me the most frightful talking to — with violent language and everything — the worst set-to I've ever had.'

'In broken English?'

'No, she spoke quite good English. She'd been with my aunt for years: a faithful German servant with a horrible, really nasty nature — I think — well, anyhow, very German: changing from one attitude to another. My aunt was not told — I don't remember her talking about it at all — but she did say in an affectionate way: "I'm very sorry, I think your parents want you home."'

'This was after only a few weeks?'

'Well, perhaps a month or so . . . Of course, my father had to be told. And Aunt Janie, his sister and Lytton's mother — oh, I had great respect for her! — she said: "What nonsense! Pay no attention to it. Boys will be boys." That was a slight comfort to my father. However, he said: "I'm going off to see Dr Hyslop who is the head of the lunatic asylum at Bedlam and I'll take Duncan with me. We'll see what he says." So off we went. I was rather nervous. We went into this vast building, which was then about a mile long, and were ushered into Dr Hyslop's room. Immediately I felt at ease. He was such a completely humane, decent sort of lively person. My father told him the story . . . One of the things the doctor in Nice had said was: "What signs does he give of not being able to finish anything? Does he take up ideas and projects and then not push them through?" My uncle replied: "Oh yes, he's always beginning pictures and then not finishing them." At this Dr Hyslop laughed and said: "I'm a painter myself in my spare time and I often begin things and don't finish them. There's nothing in that. Don't give it a thought." He altogether comforted my father. I left the place in quite a different state of mind from when we entered and I heard nothing more about it.'

'What a relief it must have been!'

'The greatest relief, but though the tension of the thing had gone on for weeks I don't remember being in the least bit worried by Uncle Trevor's goings-on. I thought he was being very stupid and I didn't at all take the view of the doctor in Nice. I hardly thought of *How We Lost Our Virginity* again after reading it. Everyone seemed to me

33

to be talking nonsense. As for not finishing pictures, I knew why I didn't finish them: it had nothing to do with going off my head . . . Well, that's the end of the story.'

'And maybe it leads straight on to another story.'

'If I can think of one, but this story's finished: there's nothing more to be said. I think it's a complete story.'

*   *   *   *   *

Our picnic in the Park, if on the frugal side, has proved delightful. We are alone except for an old Turk who wanders about the path and recesses near us sweeping. No wonder the place is so neat! Every time he passes us he gives me a benign twinkle. There is something about my relationship with Duncan which he thoroughly approves of. And he is curious. I have got out the little Agfa Instamatic camera (bought like the electric shaver at Selfridges) and begin to snap Duncan with this supposedly foolproof instrument. I steal up to him in every attitude: Duncan peeling a banana, Duncan failing to light a Marmora, Duncan hazy with drowsiness. 'Bring'm back alive,' I tell him. 'I like to get them in their natural haunts.' 'Tease!' he says, 'tease!' The old gardener comes up to me and asks if Duncan is my father. I nod and he gives a loving smile. My simplification, my innocent lie, is so much nearer the truth for both of us.

As I feared, Duncan's long morning has exhausted him. The walk to the Perge through the gardens is only about a hundred yards but those yards take him fifteen minutes to cover. There are still the three flights of stairs to our bedroom. I settle him in an armchair for five minutes and then slowly we ascend, with me lifting him from behind. Once in the bedroom, I peel off his hot, tan-coloured, brushed-cotton suit (which is really quite a cool suit, if *any* garments can be considered cool here) and naked he sinks deliciously between the sheets. As for myself, I race down the perpendicular steps of the hotel into the rock pool in the sun.

As I lie on a straw mat after a swim, with the great American warships dotting the bay with grey, my mind turns to the many conversations I have had with Duncan on the famous '*Dreadnought* hoax' he was a part of. The story is too well known to be dwelt on but the gist of it is that in February 1910, in an elaborate escapade devised by Horace de Vere Cole, a telegram was sent to the Admiralty as from the Foreign Office alerting the First Lord to the historic fact that the Emperor of Abyssinia and his retinue were on their way to Weymouth: there to inspect HMS *Dreadnought*, the biggest and newest of His Majesty's ships of line. The royal party consisted of Adrian Stephen and his sister Virginia, Duncan, Anthony Buxton, Guy Ridley, and Horace Cole. The party was made up in Fitzroy Square by Clarksons the theatrical costumers, and proceeded by train from Paddington.

'Weren't you nervous?' I asked.

'Not so much nervous as hungry. We dared not eat because of our make-up. Both

Virginia and I wore beards. I think Adrian was nervous because the admiral of the flagship was a cousin of his, and then to his horror the captain of the *Dreadnought* turned out to be someone he knew very well and used to go on long walks with. But he wasn't recognised although his disguise was of the flimsiest. He was a Foreign Office interpreter.'

'Were you royally welcomed at Weymouth station?'

'Yes, it was a great moment. A red carpet had been rolled out for us to walk on, and a crowd of sightseers had gathered at the barrier. We were conducted in cabs to the harbour and there a smart little brass-funnelled launch took us out to the *Dreadnought*.'

'It must have been unnerving being received by the Admiral and captain in gold-braided uniforms.'

'It was. Then there was a scare when a certain rating was sent for who was the only man in the Fleet who could speak Abyssinian. Luckily he was away on leave that day. Another scare was when my moustache began to peel off. Adrian, however, was very quick. He separated me from the others and pressed it back again.'

'What language did you speak?'

'Luckily Adrian did most of the speaking. He was brilliant: mispronouncing whole passages of Homer and Virgil which he'd had to learn by heart as a boy and mixing it up with a few words of Swahili.'

'Wasn't it a relief when you got back on the train?'

'We were exhausted, and the only thing we could think of was a meal. Dinner was served in our compartment, Cole insisting that the waiters wore white gloves. But he tipped everyone in princely style all along the line. I think the whole thing cost him about £300.'

'Which I suppose would be three thousand now.'

'I dare say.'

'What happened afterwards?'

'Cole, who was always out for publicity, let the cat out of the bag. There was quite a stir . . . headlines, questions asked in the House, music-hall songs, and the Navy furious. They proceeded to punish us each in turn. I was taken unawares one morning while sitting at breakfast with my parents. The maid announced that some gentlemen had called to see me. I went to the front door in my slippers, only to be tripped up and bundled into a cab. There I found myself sitting on the floor at the feet of three young naval officers each carrying a cane. "Where are we going?" I asked. "You'll see plenty of *Dreadnought*s where we're going," one of them said. I suppose I must have looked frightened because they enquired if I felt ill. They made me get out at a field somewhere and I did whatever I was told.'

'I remember,' I interjected, 'how in Adrian Stephen's account one of them said: "I can't make this chap out. He doesn't put up any fight. You can't cane a chap like that."'

35

'That is so . . . It all ended by their giving me two ceremonial taps on the behind. The honour of the Navy was seen to be vindicated and that was that.'

'What happened then?'

'They saw that I was still in my bedroom slippers and they offered to take me home. I felt I couldn't very well allow this and I went home by underground . . . They were very nice young men.'

We feel well rested and have hired a *carrozza* to take us round the town. It is Duncan's first real vision of Antalya. The timing is perfect. The sky is clear and the sun over the mountains slants across the bay. His painter's eye is enchanted with houses and gardens. Our horse and carriage amble through the crowds and come to the outskirts of the city. We halt by an ancient stone trough and the cab-man gives his horse a long drink. Duncan says to me: 'Do you think you can buy me some cigarettes? I've completely failed with these Marmora. I'm not going to have any more truck with them.'

The little shop by the stone trough sells rope, seeds, flowerpots, horses' bits, oranges and tomatoes, meal, potatoes, soap, cigarettes but, alas, not what I have been longing for for two days: pipe tobacco and cigars.

The thirst-quenched horse shows no signs of rejuvenation after his elixir and proceeds with ambulatory gait to another part of the town. I take up our guidebook and begin to read:

' "Antalya is a tourist centre of the Southern coast of Turkey: the Turkish Riviera. It has 95,000 inhabitants." '

'Yes,' comments Duncan, 'it looks as though the whole ninety-five thousand are in the streets this evening.'

The remark is justified. The place buzzes with busyness. It reminds me of Toluca in Mexico which I knew in the days of its first flush of discovering what is called 'a higher standard of living'. The shops bulged with washing-machines, refrigerators, television sets (though there was no television), factory-turned furniture, chromium fittings, a plethora of plastic in all its forms, and mass-produced pots and pans. I find the same here, but with even more chromium for there are mines of it in the mountains. I say to Duncan: 'What an enthralling place Antalya must have been only a few years ago!' 'Yes,' he agrees, 'and it's still on the whole picturesque.'

This is true. We pass small gardens glanced at through a fragment of Roman wall, or seen through a trellis of vines, with private orchards of pomegranate and mulberry, orange, walnut and fig. Here and there droops the opulent green of the persimmon. Upper storeys jut and hang, sometimes almost touching over the narrow streets. I can well imagine the atmosphere of charm, loquacity and quarrelling that must have pervaded the air in the days when a third of the population was Greek. I can see some intractable pasha sitting in state behind the shade of lattices and ministered to by Arab slaves costing seven pounds apiece. Lolling back on cushions, he drinks his sherbet and defies the central government.

' "The city dates from the second century BC," ' I read out from the guidebook as we jog along. ' "It was called Attalia, eponymously named by its founder Attalus Philadelphus, King of Pergamum, whose dynasty dominated a large part of Western Asia Minor. Its harbour though small had the advantage of the deep sweep of the bay. Before long Antalya overtook Side as the most important port in Pamphylia." '

'Side?' interjected Duncan, 'I thought that's where we're going.'

'Yes, now that I've got my bag back, we can. As a matter of fact, this morning I went to the Pamphylia Travel Service and spoke to an attractive and very efficient brunette called Sirma Subutayi. It's all arranged that the car we hired from London shall be delivered to us in Side in four days' time.'

'But do we want to stay here four days?' Duncan countered.

'By no means – though I wouldn't mind making the Hotel Perge my headquarters. Tomorrow morning at 10.30 a car is calling for us and we're being driven to Side: all for a hundred Turkish lira.'

Duncan gave one of his non-committal grunts. 'I hope you'll be there,' he said. 'Now read me more about Antalya.'

' "The Emperor Hadrian visited the town in AD 130 and made a gift of a city wall to defend the city from the Arabs. Not much more is heard of the town until the Twelfth Century when it became an important base for the Second Crusaders" . . . Oh, I see something I've missed . . . "St Paul the Apostle and his companion St Barnabas stopped in Antalya on their way to Antioch. St Paul preached in nearby Perge on his return journey, and probably in Antalya." '

'He would have!' Duncan snorted.

Our relaxed drive through the city is over. The *carrozza* has returned us to the Hotel Perge but the cab-man demands double his fee, saying we have been out double the time. This I refuse, becoming as heated as he is in a stumbling polyglot fishwives' set-to. I end up by giving him half the extra he wants. Grumbling, he leads his horse away. I take Duncan's arm and we walk down the steps to the restaurant terrace. It is sunset. The bay is a wash of rose and lilac dissolving into the mountains. We sit outside sipping our rakis and watching the daylight fade as the lights of the American Fleet come on.

'Hi there! Good evening to you both,' comes a familiar voice. It is Joe Warren. He sits down at our table and we press him to stay and dine with us.

'Thanks, but sorry. I'm expecting the Naval Attaché and a party from the Fleet to turn up and I must leave myself free to eat with them.'

A day spent with the Navy among his own kind has filled him with reassurance. He is buoyant.

'God! when I think what I've seen of this dump so far, I sure am glad I was born an American,' he says with the relief of one who has escaped a nightmare. He seems to have given some kind of account of Duncan and me to his companions and for the first time asks about Bloomsbury.

'I've read Virginia Woolf,' he tells us, 'but I didn't know that Vanessa Bell was her sister . . . And who was Lytton Strachey?'

'A cousin of Duncan's,' I answer. 'There were ten of them before two died, and their mother was Duncan's father's sister. Lytton became famous when he wrote *Eminent Victorians*.'

'Who were some of the others?'

'The originals can be numbered on two hands. There were Clive Bell and Roger Fry, both art critics. Clive wrote *Civilization* and Roger *Vision and Design* . . .'

'Oh yes, I've seen both of those in paperback recently.'

'Then, there was Leonard Woolf, the writer, and the two brothers of Vanessa and Virginia, Thoby who died in his twenties, and Adrian. Then, of course, Maynard Keynes the economist – whom you people in the States know only as Lord Keynes.'

'He was one of them, too, was he!'

'And an obscure mysterious creature, Saxon Sydney-Turner – who was brilliant, they all say – who doesn't seem to have come to anything, and lastly Desmond MacCarthy, the man of letters.'

'And Duncan?'

'Oh yes, especially Duncan. He flits in and out of all accounts of them; though to my mind he was in some ways very un-Bloomsbury.'

Here Duncan himself chips in with: 'What ever do you mean? We were *all* very different from each other.'

'Maybe, but there's one characteristic of theirs, it seems to me, that you're entirely without, though it's difficult exactly to put a finger on it because it showed itself in various guises. Sometimes it was an apparent aloofness – an intermittent chilliness – which may merely have been mood or shyness; sometimes, a terrifying air of superiority – "What *do* you mean by that?" – and sometimes, though I think this was more Strachey than anything, a way of making you seem foolish simply by repeating your last sentence with a questioning inflection in the voice . . . Marjorie Strachey whom I adored and shared a flat with for eight years was a master of this.'

I turn to Duncan. 'Say something, Duncan, anything, and I'll give you a demonstration – make you feel that what you've said is ill-considered, shallow, and possibly a little foolish.'

Duncan looked out over the dark bay, now ablaze with the lights of the American Fleet, and he said: 'What a lot of lights and ships there are!'

I gaze at him with a searching, mocking earnestness, repeat the statement as a question but with a note of incredulous emphasis on the two key words, 'lights' and 'ships': 'What a lot of *lights* and *ships* there are?'

Duncan does not want to laugh, but he does. Joe Warren and I join in.

38

'That's Bloomsbury one-up-manship for you,' I say. 'It's so simple, and always effective. It somehow takes the cockiness out of one; puts one on the defensive.'

'And that's what you say I don't do?' Duncan remarks.

'No, though you do have your own way of putting yourself on top.'

'Oh?'

'The old prep-school trick of scoring first. For instance, yesterday when I was struggling to push you up the stairs from behind, you exclaimed: "Don, stop trying to hurl me to the ground." '

Duncan, again laughing in spite of himself, turns to the young American: 'Clever as a bag of monkeys, isn't he!'

It is only 9.30 when we decide to retire, but the sea air and the warmth have made us both sleepy. We bid our goodbyes to Joe Warren and hope that his Navy friends will turn up; for he has still not eaten.

September 19th

I wake up thinking: 'There is much to be done this morning before we leave Antalya. It is our third day in a place we only expected to be for a few hours.'

Just as I am creeping out, Duncan stirs and opens his eyes; so I come back into the room and peel him a peach for breakfast.

'Where are you going?' he asks.

'To the market. I want to get a strap for my bag and look for sandals. We also need vodka, cognac and raki to take to Side. There may be nothing there . . . Don't forget that a car is coming for us at 10.30.'

'Oh God!' he says, 'and you won't be here.'

'I shall . . . Now go back to sleep or the Turks will come and get you.'

'No no, not that!'

I tuck him up and slip out into a superb morning: the sky cloudless, the air fresh with warm perfumes. I feel young. Unencumbered by black trousers – though still in socks and boots – I stride through the gardens past beds of canna and arbours of jasmine and bougainvillea.

It is not yet eight o'clock and I hope Duncan will sleep till nine, though already I picture him beginning his repertoire of searches which, like the Muslim call to prayer from the minarets, happens five times a day: spectacles, cigarettes, handkerchief, passport, sunglasses, little red diary, Midland cheque book, travellers cheques, and the silver travelling clock given him by Lydia Keynes. Each of these has become a symbol of security for him and unless they can be immediately mustered he seems to face nothingness. When we are properly organised I shall simplify the ritual by keeping all these, at all times, in a basket to themselves. Everything else – including sketchbook, charcoal, pastels, corkscrew, raki, knife, and above all Lord Kinross's *Europa Minor* — I shall dump into a large panier.

As to this last book, we have found it indispensable, but since we are two of the slowest readers in the world and seldom remember what we have read, we peruse the same passages over and over again.

I am wondering what to do about handkerchiefs. Duncan is such a moist creature — either pisces or aquarius — and he gets through them faster than I can wash them. 'Oh Duncan, you are so rheumy, so full of rheum!' 'So you say.' 'Yes, you are like a sponge.' 'Tease!' 'I suppose we shall have to rely on those awful paper things which the Americans call "tissues". We have a box of them labelled "man-sized", which they aren't in the least.'

The market is packed. It has obviously been in full swing for hours. This is my third descent upon it and I am beginning to know my whereabouts. I go straight to the cobblers' and leather-workers' lane to look for a strap. Here is an honest-looking craftsman sitting on a stool and carving a harness. I pull out my list of the Roman Emperor's shibboleths and point to the one that says: 'Do you have a strap to bind this bag together?' He shows me a strap which seems to me too long and too expensive. Our dumb charade begins.

'Do you not have a shorter? Or cut the long in two.'

'No. And the long cut in two will not be long enough.'

He pauses, takes the gutted black bag in his hands as though it were a wounded goat, runs a finger along the broken zip, nods knowingly like a great surgeon, and calls his son over to him — a boy of about sixteen — then turns to me. Would I like the zip mended? Yes yes yes! But how long will it take? About an hour. And how much will it cost? The question is obviously irrelevant and the boy has disappeared with the bag. For better or worse I am stuck for an hour. In little more than half an hour the taxi will arrive at the Perge to take us to Side. Duncan will panic. I must somehow telephone him. Pointing to a shibboleth which says: 'I shall be back in half an hour', I run to the office of the Pamphylia Travel Service (about a mile away) and beg the help of the efficient and pretty brunette, Sirma Subutayi.

'Please telephone our chauffeur and tell him not to come till 11.30. Secondly, please get in touch with Mr Duncan Grant at the Hotel Perge and let him know about the altered time.'

'Nothing easier!' she says.

Ah, she does not know Duncan! She returns with a baffled look and says: 'The first is done. The second is a puzzle. Finally I had to put down the receiver. Mr Grant gives an occasional grunt, otherwise there's absolute silence.'

Wryly, I see Duncan in my mind's eye picking up the receiver like some palaeolithic man, deciding that the timbre of voice at the other end is unknown and menacing, and refusing to risk speech.

40

Self-portrait, *c.* 1909, National Portrait Gallery

Bathing, 1911, Tate Gallery

'Please,' I say to Miss Subutayi in my most coaxing way, 'do one thing more. Telephone the Perge again and leave this message: "Tell Mr Grant — the old gentleman, the painter, the one who goes about with a sketchbook — that the car is arriving at 11.30 and not 10.30." '

Back in the street of the leather-workers, I am given a stool to sit on and a glass of hot tea. While striving to make it clear how much I appreciate such good manners without being able to say so, I am amazed by the reappearance of the boy — and with my bag — my bag perfectly mended: a brand new zip. The cost of all this? A paltry 10 lira, about 20p. Such sterling service must be rewarded, and so I buy from my leather-man several sets of handmade glass beads, such as are used in Turkey to embellish the harnesses of horses and donkeys. We part swearing allegiance, and I run all the way to the Perge.

It is all right, Duncan has been warned about the altered time. I tax him about his performance over the telephone.

'Whatever possessed you just to grunt at Mademoiselle Subutayi?'

'Call her what you like, I can't be expected to answer to a strange female,' he says.

We load up and sink back into the hired car. The suburbs are soon done with and we are heading south across the Pamphylian plain: grey-green and ochre broken by patches of rocky scrub. Far away to our left is a filmy ridge of mountains. The road — strung with small trees and the occasional cardboard village — has an even surface and is empty of traffic except for the odd taxi and lorry. I point to a field bursting all over with puffs of white.

'Duncan, look at the cotton!'

'Oh, is that cotton? I thought it was white flowers.'

'It's after twelve. Would you like a raki?'

'Of course . . . What else have you brought?'

'Cognac, vodka and wine.'

'Good!'

We both fall asleep and when I next look up everything has changed. The flat terrain has hummocked into small hills. Olive trees dot the terra-cotta earth. Aqueducts, arches and Roman walls rise up and disappear, stretching towards the sea. We are three or four kilometres from Side — it is an exciting moment — and we seem to be driving towards the centre of a ruined city.

'Oh look, Duncan, we are entering the gates!'

We pass through the great gate with its sand-coloured pillars, turn abruptly left and drive through a street of ancient colonnades under the shadow of the colosseum, whose drum is supported by enormous arches. As we proceed, all the grandeur dwindles into a dusty ramshackle village perched among ruins along the edges of the sea. We branch off left again and the taxi jolts over a stony side street, up an incline, then along the verge of a short cliff. We stop outside the only impressive building in

41

the village which is not a ruin: the Hotel Pamphylia.

'This is it,' I say. 'This is the place I arranged about over the telephone.'

'It's rather fine in its way,' Duncan answers. 'I like the arched windows.'

A woman with a distinctive bearing and a quietly commanding manner greets us in the hotel foyer. She is about sixty: grey hair, dark eyes, a Roman nose. Certainly, she is 'quelqu'un'.

'Choisissez n'importe quelle chambre que vous voulez,' she tells us regally. And then, with admirable directness and still in French, she says: 'Full *pension* is 125 lira a day, *demi-pension* 90. Would you like luncheon? . . . Very well . . . And dinner tonight? Excellent.'

I said I thought *demi-pension* would be best for us.

'Just as you wish. Let it begin tomorrow.'

We walk into the big sparse drawing-room overlooking the sea. It is a room of large arched windows and few embellishments: an enamel stove standing on slate-blue tiles, a door painted in faded gold and blue.

'This is a fine room,' Duncan remarks.

'My nephew is a painter,' Madame replies. 'He designed this room.'

'Then he must be a good painter,' Duncan tells her. We can see she is pleased.

'But it is a neglected room,' she goes on. 'When guests are not in their bedrooms they are by the sea. And yet even in the greatest heat of the day a breeze presses through these windows.

'I expect I shall be here a great deal,' Duncan says to her. 'There's a wonderful view of the sea. I can sit and paint from here.'

'Consider it your own room,' Madame replies.

Duncan takes my arm and we go up one flight of stone stairs to the bedroom I have chosen. He decides to have the bed nearest the door; I am happy with the one by the window. We drink to our new home in a pre-lunch raki. Then I run off for a quick swim.

The dining-room is outside: a large covered veranda open on one side to the sea and on the other to the garden, which grows among the ruins of what might well be a rich Sidetan's villa of the second century AD. Beautiful arches and strong walls with tall niches for statues rise up behind the simple structure, and among the ruins of these ancient and lofty rooms cannas splash red and gold, calabashes hang with rank ease, and roses mingle with marigolds and bougainvillea. Amid this summery and nostalgic beauty, we sit at a small square table facing the sea — which is just forty yards away, separated from us by a low wall, a road, and a small cliff. At a nearby table, also having lunch, sits Madame.

'Do you suppose she's a diplomat's daughter?' I suggest.

'I shouldn't wonder. She has that air. Perhaps her father was ambassador in Paris.'

'Yes, there's nothing provincial about her. I expect she knows England too.'

Has she heard us? Perhaps she understands English, for seeing me place my chair in the full sun (I am in a bathing slip), she looks up and says: 'N'imaginez pas, monsieur, que le soleil ici est le même soleil que vous trouvez à Brighton. C'est tout à fait différent. Prenez garde.'

'Merci Madame, mais mon adoration du soleil est une véritable maladie, de laquelle rien ne peut me guérir.' She laughs. Duncan and I keep our voices down from now on, though our curiosity grows. After a while I ask baldly: 'Madame, you are Turkish, are you not?'

With some hauteur she lifts her head and replies: 'But of course!'

She tells us of how she and her sister first came to Side and fell in love with the dusty, untidy village sprinkled among these magnificent Greek and Roman remains which fall away into the sea.

'It is my sister who really runs the Pamphylia: my sister and her son. But she is indisposed just now and keeping to her room. She suffers from the gout, you know.'

'There's only one cure for gout,' I say.

'What is that? She is eager for anything.'

'A week's starvation, with nothing but warm water.'

Madame throws up her hands:

'For my sister, quite impossible. She'd rather die than give up the good life. She loves her food, her wine.'

'Then just three days.'

Madame laughs.

A tall, spare, fair-haired man in his middle-thirties, clad in swimming trunks, emerges from the kitchen and goes to a table piled with underwater fishing gear — flippers, snorkels, rubber suits, goggles — and begins to tinker with a spear-gun.

'My nephew,' Madame explains to us, 'my sister's son. He is really the *patron* here. His brother is the artist who designed the drawing-room.'

We have asked for the simplest of lunches: soup, poached eggs and a tomato salad. It is brought out to us by an extremely slender, unsmiling, saturnine youth of ducal solemnity. I am immensely hungry.

'Duncan, the cooking's going to be good here. The poached eggs are perfect. A test case.'

'And the soup, too, is excellent,' he says.

Among the flowers I see sweet basil growing — my favourite herb — and I cull a few leaves for our eggs.

'What about wine?' Duncan asks.

'I've got a bottle of what we bought in Antalya — red — under the table. Dare we open it?'

'Not without asking.'

When the *patron* passes I say to him with a note of apology: 'Do you mind us

43

drinking our own wine?'

'Not at all, but one day you must try some we have here which I think is good.'

Two large women in bloomers have appeared from the kitchen; not tall women but ample, with fine eyes and oval faces: valiant women straight out of the Book of Kings. They sweep and clear and smile, gold flashing from their front teeth. Perhaps it is they who do the cooking. And now from the sea side comes another stripling, a boy of about sixteen, fair-haired, lithe, with an exquisite Ganymede face. He wears bathing trunks and is covered in sea-drops. Madame introduces him to us: 'My grand-nephew. The son of the painter. He speaks English.' The boy, aloof with shyness, hardly seems to notice us but walks as if in a dream to the table where all the snorkel equipment is assembled. 'He reminds me of Potey,' Duncan remarks.

'Yes, but Potey's robuster . . . Shall we kill the bottle?'

'Naturally . . . though it's not the world's best.'

'Let's try the *patron*'s wine at dinner tonight,' I say. 'In any case I don't think we ought to ask him if we can drink our own again.'

'No.'

All this time, I have been champing to wander through the ruins of Side and find a place to lie in the sun. Duncan is in bed for his siesta and the curtains are drawn. Judging by the way he staggered from lunch he is good for at least two hours.

The time is 1.30, the sun gloriously hot, at its peak: only a fool would be out in it. The breeze from the sea, however, keeps me cooler than I would be on an August afternoon in Aldermaston, lying on the lawn behind my screen of artichokes, or sun-trapped in Duncan's little patio at Charleston. Having found no sandals in Turkey yet, I walk barefoot over the burning dust and stones.

The road leads along the edge of the sea, past one or two wooden houses, and then becomes a path. I walk through a tall gateway into the ancient city and find myself among the ruins of the gymnasium. On all sides of me are broken pillars and prone columns, fallen marble pediments, fragments of relief and frieze, ceiling blocks of cut stone. A catalogue of the embellishments lying in a 12-yard circle around me would itself be a treasury of Greek and Roman design from the fourth century BC onwards.

The south-eastern end of the gymnasium opens – through the broken inner city walls – to a sweep of sandy bay about two miles long. Cooling my feet in the sea as I walk, I come to the outer city walls, then turn inwards, climb among the ruins, doff everything, and lay myself supine on a slab of stone. This is the moment of moments. Around me are the ruins of streets and fallen houses, their lintels and collapsed arches jutting out of the sand. Within a few yards' running distance is a sea of blue champagne and milk (as I described it in a postcard today) into which I know I can dip the moment the sun is too strong. It is no wonder that so much antiquity, so much nostalgia for things past, and the wine at lunch and the silence, and the perfumes of warm plants, send me into a slumber as heavy as the stone on which I lie.

There is a change in the air when I awake. It is still warm but the quieting of the strong sun – which leaches out colours – has made it more luminous. I immerse in the sea, towards which the shadows of old Side are now stretching in arch and column.

My apprehensions about having left Duncan so long are immediately allayed: I find him still snoring.

'What time is it?' he mumbles as I pull the curtains, letting the light – now well west over the ocean – flood in.

'Just after five.'

'No no! That's impossible. I couldn't have slept three hours.'

'Nanny says you should have, could have, and did,' I reply. 'You needed it.'

A raki each stands in for tea and then, with Duncan leaning on my arm, we set out to explore the village. Our progress is halting, our rests many. At one of them he remarks: 'She was quite right, that Italian lady' – he means Mrs Hamish Hamilton who talked to us about Turkey when we saw her at one of Lady Birley's Sussex festivals – 'when she said the ground in Asia Minor, was rough and stony.'

'All the more reason for you to lift your feet,' I retort a little harshly. 'Pretend you're marching.'

'One can't march on jagged ends,' he counters.

At last we reach the village square and make for a café overlooking the sea.

'Shall we fortify ourselves?' I suggest.

'Certainly. Why not another raki? It's becoming my favourite drink.'

'That's why you're suddenly walking so well. You've quickened your pace.'

'So you say!'

'Yes, now you're striding with fine bold steps.'

'Tease!'

We watch the sun going low over the ocean as the square fills up. We are at the hub of activities. Four cafés and restaurants, two or three shops, and the post office, abut the square. A mixed crowd of Sidetans and visitors sit at little tables under the trees. The visitors are mostly boys and girls with rucksacks at their feet. A music melancholic with quarter-tones vies with the stridency of Western pop as the light fades.

We ask a taxi-man how much he would charge to take us back to the Hotel Pamphylia, which is only about four hundred yards away. 'Ten lira,' he says. That seems to me a shocking price considering it costs only 10 lira to go to the town of Manavgat which is four miles away. The man appears shocked and puzzled when we decline him. It is only later that I discover that 10 lira is in fact the established charge for *any* journey within three or four miles of Side. As we turn away, I regret it.

Dinner at the Pamphylia proves excellent: a tossed green salad, red mullets fresh from the sea, and little kebab things buried in pastry. We ask the *patron* to give us a bottle of that wine of his he spoke of. He comes back with a Turkish burgundy. Having by now tried a good many wines in the last three days we do not expect anything shattering, but in our first sip we know that we have something outstanding: mellow enough to be ten years old, distinctive enough to come from a great grape and an exceptional vintage.

'Duncan, we're made!' I crow. 'And this is only a lira or two more than the stuff we buy from the shops.'

'It's almost too good to be true,' he says.

The *patron* looks at us with a pleased – and I cannot help thinking – a wily look.

'We have quite a lot of bottles,' he tells us.

Two new youths have appeared to wait at table: rounder and sweeter than the saturnine son of a disinherited duke, and more jovial than the silent Ganymede, but of about the same age. They have a gentle contemplative look about them and a half-smile playing about their lips. I came across one of them today playing the balalaika on the roof. Now Madame has come in, dressed for dinner in black, with a blue chiffon veil. This youth pulls away her chair for her as she bows to Duncan and me. Now he awaits her orders.

*   *   *   *   *

'Duncan, tell me again the story of Rupert Brooke and the headmaster of your first prep school . . . Rupert was a little bit senior to you wasn't he?'

'Yes, by a year or two. The school was called Hillbrow near Rugby and the head-master was a Mr Eden, whose wife Horatia was the sister of the Mrs Ewing who wrote *Jackanapes* – a famous children's book . . . though I don't suppose you've read it.'

'I'm afraid not . . . How old were you?'

'I must have been thirteen or fourteen: not older because I left the school at fifteen. Mr Eden was a funny little man who was too fond of his boys to be allowed to keep on the school.'

'I remember your telling me how he liked birching his boys.'

'Yes, he used to hum before doing it. Whenever we heard humming down the passage we all knew what it meant – a birching somewhere.'

'And were *you* ever birched by him?'

'Oh yes, he birched me several times with pleasure . . . Though he wasn't improper. He did his birching straightforwardly.'

'But there was something less proper he liked doing too, wasn't there?'

'Well, he liked visiting the little boys while they were having their baths. And he did . . . he did do . . . improper . . . gestures towards those little boys he was fond of while they were having their baths. And one of them split on him one day. This little boy's father was a master in the big school at Rugby.'

'And then?'

'And then there was a frightful scandal. It ended in poor Mr Eden's being denounced by the headmaster of Rugby and told he must leave within twenty-four hours.'

'How does Rupert come into this?'

'Rupert behaved nobly. Mr Eden had disappeared. Nobody knew where. No letters sent, no address known, nothing. And nobody seemed to care. Then Rupert discovered – I don't know from whom – that he was hiding in Liverpool. So Rupert went off to Liverpool and tracked him down; told him he must *not* be in this state of mind; he must go back to the school, pack up quietly and leave in decent order. Rupert saved him.'

'Decent order? Was he living in squalor?'

'Probably, and desperate: very near suicide, I should think. After Rupert's visit Mr Eden recovered his senses to some extent and, as far as I remember, actually came back. At least, Mrs Eden was able to get in touch with him and they made arrangements to wind up their time at the school.'

'So, Mr Eden had fled even from Mrs Eden: the Mrs Eden who was the sister of Mrs Ewing?'

'That's right, the sister who wrote *Jackanapes*.'

'What extraordinary character Rupert Brooke showed! Fancy, a boy of only fifteen or sixteen – and in those days – having the guts and imagination to do what he did!'

'I know. It was remarkable.'

September 20th

Our breakfast is hot tea without milk – which cannot be had – laced with Turkish cognac. I prepare it in our bedroom with one of those little electric immersion heaters you can drop into a cup. After breakfast, we pick our way over the rocks to the northern end of the small bay beneath the hotel, looking for a place to sketch from.

'The problem is, Duncan, where can I put you on this whole beach out of the sun?'

'There's no sun here.'

'No, but there will be in an hour or two. It'll swing round.'

Eventually I lodge him, crab-like, underneath a ledge of hanging rock. He balances on the green canvas folding stool he disdained a few days ago; his broad-brimmed straw hat which I bought for him in the market at Antalya is wedged against the ceiling of rock. Obviously this will not do, so I try planting him directly on the sand, but a few minutes later as I am drying myself from my first swim he calls to me plaintively:

'Don, it's too painful . . . Can't I sit upon a rock?'

'All right, I'll find a couple of flat rocks.'

Now he is sitting on two flat stones which I have covered with a plastic bag and a towel. Within a pace or two – and it is too late to do anything about it – I am horrified to see a lump of excreta. However, it is as desiccated as a dead dog from Pompeii. I decide to leave Duncan in blissful ignorance.

'I'm going for a long walk to the furthest end of the next bay,' I tell him. 'I'll be gone for about an hour.'

I leave him sketching, contented enough if not deliriously happy with his surroundings or with my absence. What I have not realised is that our every movement has been noted; that every eye on the beach has been fascinated by the little charade of setting him up in his crab hole. Even as I leave, I see a girl full of curiosity pick her way over the rocks to his sacrosanctum. And I am wondering what to do about it when another young lady accosts me and says in English:

'So your father is a painter?'

'Yes.'

'That is my mother over there. We are sunbathing.'

Indeed, I could hardly have missed them. The daughter has a lovely figure and the mother, covered from head to foot in sand, is as large as a grampus and as red as sunset. They want to know everything. Is not my father a wonderful old man to be painting among the rocks? He is. Are we staying in the Hotel Pamphylia? We are. How well my father is for his age! Yes, he is nearly ninety. Mother and daughter are in raptures. I notice how fair-skinned they are. They tell me they live in Ankara. The girl is an air hostess for KLM. She has a sunny and open face and the way she looks at me makes me wonder what my chances are with her.

'We go back to Ankara in two days,' she says.

'Too bad! We must meet again.'

'We are not in the Pamphylia. We have a rented room just opposite.'

The mother has gone back to rolling in the sand. It worries me. She looks like a sole in fried breadcrumbs and surely will be writhing in agony before the day is done.

'Hasn't your mother had too much sun?'

'She doesn't think so.'

'It's always more than one thinks. She must protect herself . . . Will you keep an eye on my father?'

'But of course!'

I walk and run in alternate stretches along the further bay. Already the last little string of bathers is a mile away and I take off everything, luxuriating in the air and sun. A pine wood comes close to the shore and there is a freshwater pool, a kind of stunted river, that stops a hundred yards from the sea. Its still green waters, the tangle of fallen branches, the undergrowth of unknown creepers and bushes, all give it a jungle quality which fill me with primitive longings. I must explore this place, but not now. It is already well into the afternoon and I have been gone from Duncan for nearly two

48

hours. I begin to run back along the sands. Even from a mile away, when I don my bathing slip again, I can see him still lodged in his niche. The sun does not seem to have reached him yet. What a relief! I am panting when I come up to him.

'You've been away a long time,' he says.

'I know, but I've found a kind of paradise . . . What did that young lady want of you when I was gone?'

'She proved a very tiresome person indeed – German. She made me show her all my sketches and she smeared my drawings.'

'Never mind. I like what you've done.'

He had completed his sketch: a tenuous, mystic vision of coloured waves and light-drenched air.

'I'm in a state of torture, squatting here.'

'And I've come to give you new life . . . Do you remember, today's the day we agreed you were to have your first dip in the sea?'

'Oh, no no . . . I couldn't possibly. Another day.'

'But you'll love it once you're in. And it will be so cooling. Think of the days when you scuttled in and out of the sea all day long. And you'll be given a raki afterwards.'

I help him to strip to his underpants – his only bathing gear – and together we shamble towards the sea. Nervous though he is, I know Duncan is curious and full of longings. I lead him inch by inch, his straw hat still on his head, into the gently moving waves. When the water comes up to our chests I say: 'Shall I unloose you now? I'll hold you up from underneath.' He is gasping too much to reply. His feet have left the bottom and he is huddled in a tight ball, clinging to me like a monkey.

'Duncan, relax. Everybody is watching. Show them what you can do.'

I know that though most people have gone to lunch they are gazing from their lunch tables and from their windows. His tattered underpants will make him famous in Side today. As I swirl him backwards and forwards, still knotted to my arm, he pants out between gasps: 'I'm sure I can swim. Let me go. I used to be so good.'

This I do, with some difficulty, and Duncan dips immediately and quietly out of sight. I pull him spluttering to the surface.

'Even Nanny can't go on being so cruel,' I say, 'Come, I'll float you back to shore.'

'Thank God!'

Back in our bedroom I pour Duncan a stiff raki and regale myself with an ice-cold beer. The weather is like an English heatwave in June and I am deliciously thirsty.

'Do you know, the *patron* told me simply to help myself from the refrigerator . . . any time I like . . . and keep a tally. That's trust for you!'

'Certainly . . . But aren't we going to have any lunch today?'

'Yes, tomatoes and a few black olives.'

'Is that all?'

'Well, we agreed yesterday that we only really need one meal a day — a good dinner.'

'Oh!'

We had, in fact, discussed the matter and I had told Duncan how well I felt on tomatoes and olives in Corfu when I had gone to recuperate there in 1967 after the shooting of the film *Oedipus the King*.

'I got rid of even the merest ripple of a spare tyre and have never been in such good shape for years.'

'Speak for yourself.'

I see that we must compromise. When therefore the saturnine youth asks us at table what we would like to order, I tell him: 'A tossed green salad and a couple of *oeufs-sur-le-plat* for my father; for me, some tomatoes and black olives . . . and perhaps a little bread. We will kill a bottle of wine, of course.'

As we were heading for the dining-room veranda, the air hostess and her large mother met us on their way back to the sun and the beach. Indeed, the mother was already there, rolling and floundering in the sand like a stranded salmon. Oh what a night is coming, I thought!

The daughter said to me: 'We've got a room in that white house over there: the one with the green shutters. When we go, would you like our room? It costs only 50 lira a day and the landlady is scrupulously clean. She will do anything you want and you'd have the use of the kitchen. Would you like to meet her? . . . Anyway, come for drinks this evening.'

During lunch Duncan and I discuss the offer.

'It's certainly tempting,' I say, 'comfortable and settled though we are in the Pamphylia. It does seem unnecessary to be paying for a breakfast and a luncheon which are so simple we can easily make them ourselves. Besides, even though we like the dinners here, it seems a pity not to try out some of the other restaurants in Side.'

'I rather agree, though we shall miss this quiet, friendly place.'

We try to put our finger on what makes the spirit at the Pamphylia so remarkable. 'It's individual, it's unpretentious,' I say, 'there's no taint of the genteel about it.'

'Perhaps because it's aristocratic,' Duncan answers. 'Everybody here, from Madame to the four youths, is allowed to be himself.'

'Yes, and their response to everything is personal . . . Did you see — I've eaten it now but I gave you some — that one of the valiant women from the kitchen laid out a plate of chopped basil for me? She'd obviously seen me go into the bushes yesterday to pick some . . . I can't tell you how good it was with my tomatoes.'

That evening we drink tea with the air hostess and her grampus mother. I am surprised. With all that sand rubbed into all that redness, the grampus should be raw all over — one big lacerated mess. Not a bit of it: she glows healthily with a soft apple-pink bloom. I whisper to Duncan: 'I can't understand it.'

50

We are introduced to the landlady of the prospective room: a typical Sidetan matron with oval face, strong dark eyes, a body not tall but on the opulent side, and voluminous bloomers to match. She has a magnificent set of eighteen-carat gold teeth and though her aspect is a little severe, when she smiles it is like a burst of sun.

She shows us the room. It is airy and well lit; its four large heavily shuttered windows overlook the road and the sea. The spotless floor is of synthetic green porphyry. There are two beds, each covered with a sheet.

'Well, Duncan, shall we take it? We'll save money and you'll have no stairs to climb.'

'Whatever you think best.'

It is agreed that we take possession on Saturday, September 22nd: the day our hired car is supposed to be delivered from Antalya.

*   *   *   *   *

'Duncan, I wish I had met Virginia Woolf. Though I expect I should have been terrified – or more likely, too ignorant even to be terrified . . . I vaguely remember the headlines when she was found to be missing . . . Why did she drown herself?'

'I think she felt her madness coming on again – the war got her down – and she couldn't face putting Leonard and Vanessa through all the business of nursing her back to sanity . . . I don't think she was unhappy.'

'Do you think she would simply have dismissed me as an illiterate? The only book I'd read of hers was *The Common Reader*. And that was rather above my head.'

'She loved meeting different forms of life and you would have been a form of life she'd never come across before. I think she would have been fascinated.'

'What was she like when you first met her?'

'That was very early on in her career. She was young and completely unknown and was spending years writing and re-writing her first novel *The Voyage Out*. She lived in Fitzroy Square and so did I. She shared no. 29 with her brother Adrian Stephen. It was a lovely old square with plane trees and a magnificent Adam façade. She wrote standing up, and never for more than two and a half hours in the morning, but regularly.'

'Who were the other inmates of the house?'

'Besides her brother Adrian there was Sophie Farrell their cook and Maud their maid . . .'

'Wasn't Maud the one who once remarked: "That Mr Grant he gets in everywhere"?'

'Indeed she did. My visits became pretty frequent . . . And there was also the dog, Hans, who would put out a lighted match at a party if you held it out to him.'

'He was the dog who once made a mess on the hearth-rug when Lady Strachey was paying Virginia a visit?'

'Yes, and no mention was made of the misdemeanour by either lady.'

'Was Vanessa married to Clive then?'

'Only just. They lived in Gordon Square, where the Stracheys were. Every Thursday evening they'd come – and other friends too – to Fitzroy Square after dinner. This was a continuation of those evenings which began in Gordon Square before Vanessa married, when Thoby Stephen was still alive.'

'How long did they go on for?'

'Guests used to drift in from about ten o'clock till midnight, and the last person to leave was often at two or three in the morning. There was coffee, cocoa and buns – and a little whiskey for the late-staying gentlemen . . . Those evenings are not easy to forget.'

'Did Virginia hold forth?'

'Not at all, not in those days. She was often silent, never seemed to lead the conversation and was attentive to what others said. In fact, she lived a secluded and studious life; occasionally going abroad for the Wagner Festival with her brother, or perhaps to France or Italy with the Bells.'

'Did you see a change in her as she became known?'

'Yes: or rather, an evolution. With the gradual success of her writing and her eventual fame, she became a completely different person in society. Her conversation – among those she admired or cared for – became fascinating and brilliant. Indeed, she appeared the genius she was. Her head seemed almost made of alabaster, glowing from within with incandescent intelligence.'

'Was she witty?'

'Very. And she could be biting – could frighten as well as charm.'

'What was her voice like?'

'I found it magical: full of resonance and unexpected cadences . . . I remember a young American – it was George Bergen the painter – saying that he had never heard English so beautifully spoken. There was never any preciousness in her way of talking. In fact, the turn of her phrases had to follow the quick flowing nature of her thought. What she expressed was already limpidly clear.'

'Did she go in for intellectual people?'

'Not at all. Her intimate friends were by no means all intellectual. She chose intellect with great reserves. What she valued in her women friends was above all character and lack of pose or selfconsciousness. Perhaps as she was herself conscious of so many things she enjoyed it never seemed necessary to pretend. She wanted people to be real. If she ever gave anyone a grilling it was when she suspected they were not.'

'Did she ever give you a grilling?'

'No, I don't think she did.'

'She must have thought you were real.'

September 21st

A curious episode happened this afternoon, one that intrigued Duncan when I told him about it. I had finally discovered the perfect sunbathing place: a twelve-foot slab of stone on the very top of the south-western outer wall of Side. A hundred yards to the south was the sea. On the inner sides of the wall, below my eyrie, were the ruins of an ancient street buried in sand. On the outer side, looking east towards the River Melas (to give it its classical name), stretched a Sahara of sand-dunes sparsely dotted with shrubs. This gave way to fields of cotton and then to the pine forest I discovered yesterday. The street side of my wall was not difficult to climb because the sand swept up to it, but on the Sahara side there was a drop of about twenty feet. The slab of stone lay across the top of the ruined wall and at right angles to it, overhanging the wall on both sides and giving one the sensation of being suspended.

It was a glorious spot, bathed in a sluice of air even on the hottest days and commanding a quadruple view: the little ramshackle village dominated by the Hotel Pamphylia, the centre of the Greco-Roman town, the surrounding sand-dunes, and the sea. I found that by erecting a low parapet of stones round the edges of my slab I could stretch out naked, exposed and yet not seen.

I had left Duncan lying on his bed covered with a sheet and the breeze pouring into the room through the drawn curtains. I knew that the wine at lunch and the cognac which followed would keep him slumbering for two hours. I hurried out into the dazzling light, and ran past the now familiar tumbled columns and over the scorching sands to my airy pedestal.

Hardly had I anointed myself and experienced that first delicious stretching out in the sun (my head covered with Duncan's straw hat), when I heard a shout, gay and buoyant, coming from the Sahara side of the wall. I sat up and saw a youth beckoning to me, greeting me, and then come bounding like a puppy over the sands towards me. It was as though he knew me. Skirting the seaward end of the wall he came around and was soon standing beneath me on the street side. He climbed up the slope of sand to just below my slab and smiled up at me.

With that smile of his my heart leapt and my mind quickened to something inexplicable, uncanny — narcissistic if you like — but overwhelming: a flash of nostalgia, homage, recognition. This youth was *me*, my double: not as I was now but as I was some thirty years ago; or rather, what I would have been had I been truer to my destiny. He was, therefore, without flaw where I was marred; but the contours were the same, the attitude of body the same, the texture of the skin, the auric colouring, the shape of the face, even the spirit looking out from the light-blue eyes — all the same. This was no vague association or envious wish of vicarious juvenescence. It was the certainty of identity. I knew it in that glance: an identical style, his as naively fresh and innocent as mine once was, yet with that unexpected satyr twist to it, that

53

half-faun-half-angel gaze, half heaven, half earth, which had kept me forever trying to find Christ in Apollo and the saints on Mount Olympus. I was humbled, I was stunned.

He stood with his feet apart, wriggling his toes in the hot sand and looking up at me – speaking in Turkish. He wore a bathing slip and though I was still naked his eyes showed no surprise. I know no Turkish but I understood what he was saying. 'Come and swim with me.' 'Yes, I will.'

I climbed down from the wall and together we ran towards the sea. 'I could be running with my once young shadow,' I thought. His bare feet flew over the sand so lightly they could have been winged. We sported in the waves for perhaps fifteen minutes, standing or treading water every now and then to communicate. Then, true to that insidious impulse which drives me to sever relationships just as they are forming, I told him I had to go. I gestured towards my wall, inviting him there, but it was too late, the spell was broken. He radiated a dionysiac smile, waved, and went leaping away over the sands.

I am as prepared to believe that none of this happened as that this was no mere human stripling who bounded into my ken on that magic afternoon among the ruins of a Greco-Roman town. Angel, double, god or satyr, to what purpose had he come? If he was Hermes, with what message for my future? Fool, fool, why did you dismiss him? My eyes scanned the shore. He had run into oblivion. I never saw him again.

When I told Duncan about it after his siesta and asked what on earth had made this young creature single me out in the wilderness, he said: 'Because he recognised you, felt drawn to you.'

'What do you mean?'

'He saw someone he could instantly trust and understand.' Then after a moment, Duncan added: 'And he saw somebody whose beauty matched his own.'

'But he was far more beautiful than I ever was.'

'I think your modesty is unwarranted.'

That was the end of it. Every afternoon I wondered if I should see the apparition again. I never did . . . As I returned to my pedestal I cursed the fact that for once I had forgotten my camera. A photograph would have been the test. Preternatural beings, they say, are not amenable to cameras or to mirrors.

I lay down again in the sun and was hardly asleep when a very different kind of vision thrust itself upon me: a goat-like thing, fully clothed, came prancing on the wall towards me. It approached my slab uninvited and stood leering down at me. It was about twenty-five: coarse where the other had been delicate and strong, thick and stupid where the other had been mercurial and swift; covetous where the other would ask for nothing and refuse nothing. The grin on its goat face was lascivious.

Seizing Duncan's straw hat, he plunged it on his head. A puff of breeze lifted it and spun it down the valley. He ran off to retrieve it. I saw him pick it up, I saw his quick look at me from behind a ruin, and I saw him vanish. Dumbfounded, I sat there. Then my anger took hold of me. Why should Duncan be deprived of his straw hat? Straw hats were not easy to find in Turkey and he used his all the time. I stood up on the wall.

There was no sign of the creature on the Sahara side, nor along the shore. This meant that he must have dodged under the lee of the southern wall parallel with the sea – the one short stretch of coast my eyes did not command – and I knew that if I was quick I could head him off.

Pulling on my slip, I ran obliquely north among the ruins and suddenly came out on the sands only a few yards from where the thief was ambling along wearing Duncan's hat. There was no escape for him. Even so, I knew I must allow him to save face. It might be dangerous to accuse. I must not even ask. I walked up to him, therefore, smiling broadly as if to renew a much desired acquaintance. He smiled back as broadly and as deceitfully, doffing the hat in a wide gesture and holding it out to me. I accepted it nonchalantly and sat down with him on the sand, a pace or two from the sea. Near us a beautiful young couple lay almost naked side by side. The goat saw them and lechery seemed to drip from his coarse moustache. Leering towards them he snatched Duncan's hat and, using it as a screen, took out his thick uncircumcised penis and jerked and stretched it in their direction. That was when I pretended another minute bareheaded would strike me down with sunstroke. I got to my feet, made a grab at the hat, clamped it on my head and fled over the sands.

September 22nd

This is an exciting day. Not only is our hired car to be delivered from Antalya, but this morning, this very moment, we move from the Hotel Pamphylia to our new home a few houses away. Indeed, even now, I have established Duncan on a perch of rocks and towels to sketch the bay through a gap in the trees while I go off and execute our exodus. The *patron* is not about, so I have told Madame that some time during the day a hired car is going to arrive from the Genco Car Hire Service in Antalya. She says she quite understands.

It is 10.30 a.m. The tiresome business of moving is done, Duncan is relatively happy on his rock. My one desire is to explore that jungle backwater river I came across two days ago.

Racing past the last bathers strung out in twos and threes along the bay, I leap forward feeling as free as a Greek athlete. And now, as I strike out away from the shore, the heat of the sands on my bare feet is so great that I bless the dwarf bushes and spring from shadow to shadow. I come to a path between the pine trees and the cotton fields and then, suddenly, to that mysterious stopped-up river: a place delicious with stillness and neglect, like a forgotten garden. Fallen tree trunks loll in a water whose olivine translucence catches the movements of strange birds higher up mysteriously calling. I glimpse and hear sun-gazing turtles plopping from their logs, and the flute-noted ouzel – disturbed from deep retreats – falling in festoons of flight through the shade. All this haunting is only a hundred yards away from the vigorous simplicity of the ocean.

Blended into a recess on the opposite bank is the dim figure of a young man fishing. I edge past him hidden by tall grasses and a profuse convolvulus of an overwhelming mauve as brilliant as scarlet. I lean over the water and gather some of its seedpods, wondering how they will fare in Aldermaston without this heat and clarity of light. On my left is a field of cotton and for the first time since my childhood in India I touch this incredible plant. These are stunted, some hardly a foot high, growing in clay baked to a shard, yet bursting all over with their bolls of white. Some are in flower – a curdling of cream with orange and red – and I am struck how like hollyhocks they are. Is cotton only a mallow? And is it an annual or perennial? These are questions that will have to wait till I get back to an encyclopaedia in England. They are too weighty for me to handle in French with Madame.

I have been away from Duncan too long. After a dip in the sea I run dripping along the shore towards the Pamphylia. There he is in the distance, still sketching under the fig trees in his underwear: *my* small white football shorts which I persuaded him to exchange for his hot brown trousers.

'There you are at last,' he says. 'I'm cramped and dying of thirst.'

'What would you like: wine, beer, raki? You can have your heart's desire.'

'So you say! Give me a raki.'

I inspect his sketch, which has caught the sunlit vision of the bay looking towards Cyprus.

'Did you *have* to put that large rock in the forefront?' I ask. 'I would have left it out.'

'So you would.'

'But one can't tell whether it's a person stooping or a tombstone.'

'I can't help that. It looks like both.'

Our new lodging is only forty yards away and I am soon back at his side with a raki for him and an ice-cold beer for me. There is still no sign of our hired car.

After lunch I find the *patron* of the Pamphylia walking about in his swimming togs and fussing with snorkels and spear-guns.

'I'm still expecting a hired car,' I tell him. 'Do you mind if I wait for it up on your roof? I don't want to miss any sun.'

'Of course you may,' he answers nonchalantly, 'but a car came this morning – driven all the way from Antalya. They were asking for the name of "Roche", but we

The Tub, 1912, Tate Gallery (Copyright Angelica Garnett)

Girl at the Piano, 1940, Tate Gallery

said we knew nobody of that name here and nothing about a car . . . The man drove the car back to Antalya. It was a nice little car – white.'

I am furious with myself for never having told the establishment my name; furious with the *patron* for not putting two and two together (after all, I did tell Madame), and furious with the driver for not making further enquiries. But is there any point in showing anger? The *patron* in a desultory way goes through the motions of trying to ring up Antalya.

I sit down in the shade fretting. Is anything happening? The telephone, for all I know, is dead. Now the *patron* sits down. Madame is there and the painter-brother whom we have not yet met, as well as other members of the family. They linger over luncheon. I go over to them and say with meek reasonableness: 'Do you think the telephone call is going through?' Nobody stirs. I sit down wondering why am I not in the sea or asleep in the sun? After twenty minutes I go over to the luncheoners' table again and can think of nothing better to say than: 'The Genco Car Hire Service was under contract to *deliver* the car to us at the Pamphylia.'

The *patron* looks up languidly and replies: 'But they did. And you weren't there. Now you'll have to go to Antalya yourself to get it.'

The superciliousness of the remark makes me seethe but I remember how in Mexico one never got anywhere unless one played it cool. Turkey is probably the same. Never show anger unless you are in a position to crush. I thank him for trying to telephone and walk away from the company.

'What worries me,' I say to Duncan after our siestas as we sit on the edge of our beds drinking tea laced with cognac, 'is that so far you've seen nothing of Side, and I was going to take you everywhere in our car.'

Duncan is still in the middle of a dream. He gazes through me and says: 'Can you tell me what size sheep is?'

I play up to him: 'What kind of sheep?'

'An ordinary household sheep.'

'Oh, Duncan, don't you realise that this car hire service probably only has three cars and now someone else will get ours?'

He pulls himself together. 'It may be a blessing in disguise. Your own family doesn't rate you very highly as a driver.'

'I know. That's why I arranged it all behind their backs. Young Pote had the cheek to *forbid* me to drive.'

'He would, but I always feel safe with you.'

What I do not tell Duncan are the menacing dreams I have been having. We are driving in the wilderness. Every tuft of marram grass is real. The car stalls. The heat of the day becomes impossible. A party of red-eyed Turks pass us, stop, bait us. Duncan is assaulted, not once but over and over. Duncan is dying. He begs me to fly. I leave him dying. I have escaped but an image of him dying in the desert sears me. My name is now a byword in Bloomsbury and I eke out the rest of my life in a small village in Mexico.

'Where will you sketch this evening?'

'Not too far away,' he says.

Just as we are sitting down by a Roman arch overlooking the hotel, the *patron* hurries into the little garden beneath us and shouts: 'The car has come. Look, over there!'

True enough, a dirty red Fiat is parked outside the veranda. My heart leaps but I dislike it on sight. Why could it not have been the white one? This car is sinister.

The young man who has brought it from Antalya hands over the keys.

'How are you going to get back?' I ask him.

'By bus from Manavgat.'

'Shall we give you a lift to Manavgat?'

'Please.'

I return to Duncan jubilantly. 'We've got our car. Let's go for a drive.'

'But where?'

'Manavgat, the next town. We'll take the driver to his bus. I'll let him drive and I'll take good note of everything!'

We move gingerly away over the needle-sharp village road, but once on the tarmac, glide past the old walls, the great gate, the colonnades and the aqueducts. It is 5.30 on a golden afternoon. The breeze that presses past us is as cool as the watermelon we devoured at lunch. One last thing I ask the driver before he leaves us at Manavgat is to have the petrol station fill the tank. We say goodbye. And now for the first time I am at the wheel of a car in Turkey. Duncan is relaxed, the road is excellent, the traffic non-existent. By the time we slip through the great gates of Side again at sunset, ready for our drink before dinner, life indeed seems too good to be true.

September 23rd

Yesterday we dined at the Pamphylia, just to keep our hand in there, and were rewarded by the appearance of Madame's sister: tall, aristocratic, swathed in green silk, aged about sixty. Her elegant neck was topped by a head of silver hair, her eyes were wide apart and she had a Roman nose. Duncan and I paid our homages in French. The two sisters bowed back and the new Madame took her place at the head of the table.

It is now just on ten in the morning. The day is hot. We are in our dirty red Fiat jolting out of Side towards the museum.

'Does the name Side mean anything?' Duncan asks me.

'Yes, apparently, a pomegranate. Though it's not the ordinary word in Greek.

Perhaps it's Pamphylian. Side seems to have been founded between 1000 and 700 BC by Aeolian Greeks who gradually merged their language with the natives'.'

'You know a lot!'

'It's all in our books. Apparently there are three texts of this unknown tongue, carved in stone and found among the ruins. They date down to about the third century BC and two of them have Greek translations.'

We walk to a bench and Duncan sits. 'Tell me more,' he says.

I read, skipping and telescoping. 'After Alexander's conquest of Pamphylia in 333 BC Greek became the language of Side. Under the Romans Side became a rich commercial city and possessed a fleet. She flirted with the slave trade and allowed the pirates who plied it to use her harbour as a dockyard. Rome at first connived in this collusion with piracy. It was too good a business to let go; and the slave-market in Side became one of the most important in the world.'

I turn to Duncan. 'Isn't it amazing to think that these wharves and quays once teemed with slaves?'

'It is indeed. But I seem to remember Pompey doing away with them all.'

'Well, he did away with the *pirates*. In AD 67 in one brilliant campaign, he swept them from the seas; though they were back again by the end of the century, when Roman authority began to decline.'

'What happened to Side?'

'She had one more burst of glory in the fifth and sixth centuries with the coming of the Byzantines.'

'I don't wonder. The Byzantines are a glory in their own right. I remember my first visit to Ravenna. The mosaics were a revelation.'

'You were very young. It must have been in 1910 when you went to Greece and Constantinople with Maynard.'

'I think it must have been about then.'

'But you'd already been influenced by the portraits of Greco-Roman art . . .'

'Oh yes, I'd already seen the frescoes in Pompeii and Herculaneum. They made a great impression on me and taught me a lot about design, and also about simplicity and solidity.'

'Since we seem to have switched on to painting and art, you can tell me a few other things . . . In your student days in Paris, what were the main things you learnt?'

'Where can I possibly begin? . . . I suppose I learnt to *look* at things, to see forms and colours not merely as they appeared but as if they were part of a design.'

'A lesson you didn't fully learn till you'd seen a lot more of Cézanne, and to a lesser extent Matisse?'

'That's right. From them I learnt to organise visual experience so that line, form, and colour all became one design . . . but they weren't the only ones.'

'There was Simon Bussy. What did you learn from him?'

'Many things. He impressed me with his industry and his honesty. A painter had to paint every day no matter what he felt like.'

'Not sit back and wait for inspiration, you mean?'

'No, but keep regular hours. That was the only way of dealing with inspiration when it came. One could have days of just making a mess of things. It didn't matter. In the end discipline paid off if one made a habit of it.'

'You certainly learnt that lesson well. Discipline with you is a reflex action: out with your little stool before breakfast in Venice, Perugia, Florence, Paris . . .'

'Now now, no teasing!'

'I'm not teasing. I'm praising you . . . at your easel at Charleston every morning come rain come shine. Anyway, what else did you learn from Simon Bussy?'

'The value of copying. He encouraged me to copy the old masters: the Masaccio frescoes in the church of Santa Maria del Carmine in Florence, the portrait of Federico da Montefeltro in the Uffizi, and lots of other things. I'm in no doubt that knowing what the masters have done is the best way of learning and going on to new things.'

'What else?'

'Simon made me see that it wasn't enough to put together the harmonious elements of a composition, one had to focus them and fuse them into a whole. "Every picture should have somewhere in it *un clou*," he used to say: a point which pins the whole design together . . . But you mustn't try to pin me down as to what I learnt in Paris. The whole thing was such a continuous process, beginning before I went to Paris and going on long afterwards.'

We have risen from our seat and resume browsing through the museum. There are inscriptions, statues, columns, pots, jewellery, pavements. Under the Byzantines the city of Side expanded beyond its furthest limits, another forum was built and the theatre repaired. The Bishop of Side became tenth in importance after the patriarch of Constantinople, with fifteen bishops under him.

'Did they go to the theatre?' Duncan asks with an irreverent twinkle.

'Yes, but not for plays. They used it, apparently, as a sanctuary. That's a far cry from its days of gladiators and wild beasts! But by this time Side was settled by Jews.'

'*Your* people!'

'Maybe, but yours at that time were savages.'

'Noble savages!'

'With long noses.'

I know I can always spark off a reaction from him with the banality of a schoolboy remark. 'The old jokes are the best,' I say.

'So I see!'

As we walk back to the car I complete our potted history of Side.

'By the seventh century the city is under attack from the Arabs and its ultimate decline sets in. By 1200 it is uninhabited and in ruins . . . Did you know that the present village was started only in the 1900s? The Greeks here were shipped lock, stock, and alpha-gamma-delta back to Greece in exchange for Muslims from Crete.'

'Perhaps that's why they lack sparkle,' Duncan comments.

'Maybe, with an alien history they just "graze their herds among the broken columns and pedestals of the slave-market: an arcaded agora of imposing size", as Lord Kinross says.'

After our siestas today – Duncan prone under his sheet, me prone and sometimes supine on my slab in the sun – we drive out to explore the northern bay: a three-mile stretch of shore, the road itself but a track in the sand. It is bordered all along by a succession of jerry-built beach-huts on stilts, as rickety as the huts of aborigines and all of them empty. These peter out and give way to a drive which leads to the gardens of the Hotel Turtel. Here we get out of the car, pleasantly surprised to find that the architect has done a good unobtrusive job. The hotel, instead of rising into the sky in the prescribed cuboid stridency – throwing the coastline out of scale – is carefully terraced to blend into olive trees and gardens.

We settle ourselves on the veranda facing the sea. The light over the sea is opalescent as the sun dips towards the horizon.

'Duncan, do you think that small boys can be cruel? I remember seeing a photograph of you when you were about six, taken probably in India. You were dressed up as Cupid. A more touchingly innocent small thing it's hard to imagine. How did this guileless morsel fare in the rough-and-tumble of the prep school?'

'My first term at Hillbrow was a great success. I used to tell the boys stories about India and they all thought me delightful. Then some nasty little brat – jealous no doubt – started the idea that "Grant goes on and on about India" and they all turned against me.'

'Were you tormented?'

'Very much tormented, till I was clever enough to discover one was left alone if good at games. So I made up my mind to be good at football.'

'And were you?'

'Yes. Then they all had to respect me again.'

September 24th

We are bumping out of Side on our way to Manavgat to change travellers cheques. Though the heat is intense, I do not worry about Duncan because the breeze, so long as we keep moving, is delicious.

Manavgat is about six kilometres from Side. Twenty years ago it must have been a picturesque and typical Turkish village. Now it is a small town bristling with upstart buildings. Shops overflow with bales of shoddy which probably come from Lancashire, with ploughs and fertilisers, plastic shoes, enamelled w.c.s, radio sets, cheap lampshades and electric kettles . . . all part of the need to cater for peasants, farmers, and the new middle class which is avid for symbols of respectability and progress. Meanwhile, the magnificent Manavgat river – the old classical Melas – continues to roll its greeny-blue ice-grey waters under the bridge. Some ten miles north of the town (having flowed for hundreds of miles through chill caverns under the mountains) it gushes into the sunlight.

It being a Monday morning, the streets teem. One would think every person in Pamphylia has decided to come to town today to buy something or sell something or simply look on. The bridge over the river is a river itself: a twin river of people flowing in opposite directions. Its current is sluggish, at times stagnant. I inch our red Fiat through a flotsam of goats, chickens, barrows, carts, cars, people, and a limbless beggar on a home-made trolley – grateful that Duncan himself is not submitted to the ordeal. On the other side, what a relief it is to draw up outside the first bank we come to! It is called 'Bankasi Anadalou'.

'I won't be long, Duncan. Contemplate the passing show.'

'I dare say we are something of a show ourselves,' he says.

Once inside the bank, I announce cockily: 'I want to change some travellers cheques. What is the pound sterling today?'

'We don't handle travellers cheques. For that you have to cross the river.'

'That's exactly what I've just done.'

'Sorry, we can't help you.'

I come back to the car and find Duncan sitting in an oven.

'Never mind Duncan, we'll soon have the breeze again.'

I turn the ignition key. Not a whisper. I switch the key back and forth. There is not even the gurgle of a dying battery. I wait, try again; wait, try again. Nothing. What do we do now? To introduce Duncan to the animal flotsam on the bridge seems unthinkable. To go on sitting where we are is to die by solar frying. I am tempted to panic. Until I have changed cheques we do not even have enough money for a taxi, and what if the next bank says – as so often happened in Antalya – 'Sorry, the pound has fallen again. We can't deal in it today – not until headquarters tell us the new rate.'

Duncan waits patiently. In the calmest, most matter-of-fact way, I declare: 'There's nothing for it. We must abandon the car. Come.'

Very soon we are a humble part of that slowly moving cloaca we have so lately driven through in state. Duncan is feeling the heat. He is only just able to walk. Alternatively, I coax and scold him, assuming my monstrous role as 'Nanny'. 'Now now, master Duncan, you're shuffling. Lift your feet. Big bold steps. That's better, much better – we're almost there.'

'This is my idea of hell,' he murmurs.

At last we are in the bank and I have found him a seat. What is more, after a terrifying series of requirements, the ritual of changing travellers cheques is mercifully completed. We have no car but at least we have money. We walk slowly to a café swarming with Manavgatians. The place is noisy, dusty, hot.

'You have a raki here,' I say, 'and I'll go and telephone the car-hire people in Antalya and tell them their car is sitting outside the Bankasi Anadalou.'

'Deserting me again.'

'Just to make a quick telephone call.'

Glancing back, seeing the hunched figure of Duncan under his enormous hat, the lost look, and the Manavgatians milling around him as if he had dropped from Mars, I feel a pang. His life-enhancing presence, his mere appearance, baffles them. Even a rare American stands there staring as if he had come upon a white man among the Wai-Wai in deepest Brazil.

I have waited for twenty minutes at the post office for my call to go through, and at last I am on the line to Antalya.

'Could I speak to Miss Sirma Subutayi? It's most important.'

Gurgle-gurgle-gurgle croak-gurgle-croak.

I repeat my request in French . . . It's no use. I cannot understand nor be understood. To my horror when I return to Duncan I find him sitting in the full sun.

'Oh Duncan, and you don't even have a raki!'

'I couldn't make the boy understand.'

We move to a table inside the café: as frenetic as the bourse during a crisis but a few degrees cooler.

'I'm going in search of a belt for you.'

'What, not again?'

'I'll only be gone a minute. Console yourself with your raki.'

Ever since we arrived, Duncan's progress over Turkish ground has not been helped by one hand having to be on constant duty holding up his trousers. We forgot to pack the comfortable elastic belt Freda Berkeley (wife of the composer) gave him in London, and his only support all these days has been a thin piece of string. The car has landed us in a crisis but at least I shall find him a belt. And I do, in the third shop I try: one made of plastic, but a belt. What is more, in the shop opposite I come upon sandals: made of rubber, yes, but sandals. On the way back I risk another twenty-five minutes at the post office trying to get hold of Sirma Subutayi in Antalya. It is no good. She is not there. Meanwhile, back in the café, I find Duncan on his second raki.

'To hell with the car,' I tell him. 'Let's just abandon it and get a taxi home to Side.'

There is a new problem. Duncan is in good spirits but he cannot stand. I have to haul him into the taxi. To the crowd's delight he genuflects on the kerb and when stuffed into the taxi sits on the floor. No matter, we are speeding out of Manavgat. It is like fleeing from a burning city.

Heavens be thanked! Two things have happened during lunch which make us feel better. Duncan was half-way though his *oeufs-sur-le-plat* and I my black olives and tomatoes, at the Pamphylia, when the *patron* managed to get Antalya on the line. It was not Sirma Subutayi but a kindly-sounding gentleman who spoke English. 'Get a garage to mend the car,' he said, 'and we'll pay you back whatever it costs.'

The other good thing is this. Hardly had I put the receiver down when the *patron* came to me and said: 'I know just the man to mend the car. A friend of mine and he comes here all the time.'

Almost at the same moment a young man appeared whom I had often seen at the Pamphylia, sometimes in the kitchen, sometimes on the fringes of the family table. He was dark, curly-haired, taciturn and solid. We were introduced. This was Ibrahim Cezir, the mechanic.

So everything is now arranged. Ibrahim Cezir is to work on the Fiat immediately. I say to Duncan as I cover him with a sheet in our cool heavily shuttered room: 'Now we can have our siestas in peace.'

'I think we've earned it,' he replies.

September 25th

Last night we were invited to a small party in Duncan's honour. It was charming. A young Turkish couple holidaying from Ankara and living in the same house but higher up than us have fallen in love with him. They are a beautiful couple: she with a fresh honey-and-peaches complexion, he – a draughtsman by profession – tall, dark and dimple-chinned with warm brown eyes set far apart. I have spoken to them both several times in our shared kitchen, and yesterday they asked me if Duncan would consider coming up the banisterless flight of stone steps to their apartment.

'I want so much to present him with a bouquet of flowers,' the young man said.

Well, in the evening soon after six it all happened. A somewhat older couple were there too. I have sometimes parleyed with them in kitchen French and broken English over the brewing of tea or the frying of an egg. He is a Turk and she a German: she ample and Rubensesque, with an open sunny countenance, he more shadowy, smaller, meeker, sweeter.

The tall dark draughtsman presented his bouquet to Duncan with exquisite shyness. He must have robbed half the window-boxes of Side to cull such a bunch of canna, geraniums, marigolds, hibiscus and bougainvillea.

He whispered to me: 'I admire him so much . . . the way he applies himself morning and afternoon . . . and such an air of courtesy surrounds him.'

Duncan was touched by the gift of flowers. He not only took them to dinner with him at the Pamphylia afterwards but insisted on bringing them back to our room.

Madame seemed to have caught the mood of homage too, for when we approached she rose from her chair, took Duncan by the hand and herself led him to our table.

'What did you talk about last night at the party?' Duncan asks me over breakfast. 'You seemed to be going at it as if nothing would stop you.'

'I know, though I thought I'd got off to a bad start. The Rubensesque Bavarian — or whatever she is — took my breath away by her opening remark. "I'm well aware that the English hate all Germans," she said.'

'And were you honest?'

'What could I do but stammer out: "Oh yes, but not all — only some"? However, she gave me such a radiant smile that I think we are forgiven.'

'What else?'

'I launched into a disquisition on the pollution of the seas, the quality of life in London, the importance of the artist, the ruinous economics of usury . . .'

'My word, no wonder I was left in peace!'

'I asked our host if anybody took any notice of the muezzin's call to prayer five times a day. "Only simple people," he replied. Then I said: "What a pity the sounds that come from the minarets are now only recordings!" "Ah, but the shepherds and farmers and peasants are far more impressed with a record than the real thing," he said. "In Turkey the only believers are the uneducated." Do you think this young man is a first-generation Turkish Bloomsbury?'

Duncan gave one of his hesitant chuckles. 'I'm not sure I like the tone of that remark.'

'Come on, you know very well how anti-religious you all were!'

'Well, I remember the arguments you used to have with Marjorie* about catholicism.'

'She was impossible. One could never begin to guess what conclusions she'd draw from a premiss. Once I gave her the autobiography of St Thérèse of Lisieux to read, thinking this would move her. Instead she was profoundly shocked and delivered me a lecture on the cruelty of the Church to nuns.'

Duncan laughed. 'Dear old Gumbo, she was quite unpredictable but a sport. And one could laugh at her . . . Do you remember the time she boiled a tin of spaghetti on the stove and it exploded on to the ceiling at Taviton Street?'

'And it remained there for eight years — the whole time I lived with her . . . And the number of times she called the fire brigade to deal with a burning saucepan!'

This morning with a chink of light splintering through the shutters and Duncan still

---

* Marjorie Strachey: one of Lytton's four sisters.

motionless under his sheet, I lay in bed thinking of that moment during last night's party when his gentle voice broke through a lull in the conversation. It is not what he says but the way he says it that I find so difficult to describe. There is a hesitant lilt to his voice, which though not strong is resilient and young. One does not think of his approaching ninety years. I remember again his saying how Virginia Woolf's voice when she was animated was shot through with incandescence and her whole head seemed to glow like alabaster. Duncan's tones too have some quality of light: the timbre though delicate and faun-like is buoyant and clean. His articulation comes in little freshets and starts, hesitant then musically running. I can only think of a brook in a wood, flecked with sun as it races.

* * * * *

'Duncan, when your mother took you off to Florence at the age of eighteen or so, it seems to have been quite a large party.'

'Yes, it included Ethel Maitland and her daughter Helen, who later married Boris Anrep the artist, and a Colonel and Mrs Foster with their daughter Naomi. The Colonel had a beautiful wife from the West Indies, a Creole with all the charm of a Creole. She was called Ethel too. Colonel Foster, however, was miserable because he'd just finished his love affair with Dorothy Strachey, who'd gone off to get married to Simon Bussy.'

'What about Naomi?'

'A lovely girl of seventeen or eighteen and run after by all the young men in Florence. She flirted with officers of the highest families: all Medicis or Strozzis or people with historic names. Once she made me tell everyone that she was confined to her room with a headache while she went off gallivanting with some young man.'

'Where did you stay in Florence?'

'All at the same hotel, the Bertolli on the Lungarno, quite close to the Ponte Vecchio. Further up the Lungarno, my mother's cousin Mrs Ewbank had taken a flat with her three daughters. Then from Liverpool, also to winter, came the Brooke girls, cousins of Rupert Brooke.'

'Did he appear too?'

'He appeared but not for long. We all used to meet in the evenings at a café – a whole party of young people – and sometimes there were picnics and expeditions.'

'With lively conversation?'

'Always that, always talk, and sometimes violent disagreements – quite natural to the young. But they were intelligent and well educated. One of the Brooke girls came all the way from Liverpool to study Dante. She grew into a scholar with a name.'

'Was Bernard Berenson in Florence then?'

'He lived just outside.'

'And was he putting Ruskin in his place?'

'Well, I thought Ruskin sentimental after Berenson, talking about unnecessary things, whereas Berenson kept very much to the point . . . In those days I thought he was a good influence.'

'But not later?'

'I became suspicious.'

'About what?'

'I can't go into it all here but you know the time many years later when I went to Florence with Vanessa and Maynard – who'd earned us enough money for the trip by his clever manipulations of money – and Berenson mistook me for Maynard and treated me like a king . . .'

'And you let him go on thinking it even when you said goodbye?'

'Yes, it had gone on for too long to disabuse him.'

'I remember the story: all was eventually discovered and you were punished.'

'Yes, there was a big return dinner and Vanessa and I were in disgrace. We were put at the bottom of the table.'

'I remember another story you once told me too, how at some do at I Tatti Berenson caught you coming out of a certain room and was furious.'

'Indeed he was. "Nobody is allowed in that room," he said. Then I asked quite innocently why a certain painting which before had been labelled, I think, Giorgione, was now ascribed to Titian. I can't remember what he said but he was a good deal put out . . . He'd got to such a point of eminence that a few syllables dropped from his lips could change a picture's value by several thousand pounds.'

'To return to your earlier Florence days – what was your love-life then? Weren't you tempted by any one of that plethora of girls?'

'No. If anything, it would have been Helen Maitland, but I can't say I tried very hard.'

'Did you make many friends?'

'Many acquaintances and one or two friends. There was a young German who, like me, was copying at the Uffizi. We met one day while both gazing at the Arno. He was elegant and obviously rich, because a servant carried his paintbox. He took me driving in an open carriage round the Cascine Gardens – which was the fashionable thing to do at about four in the afternoon. One day after talking about a book he was reading he suddenly asked me: "Are you an *homme-femme* or a *femme-homme*?" I found that difficult to answer.'

'*Homme-femme*? Do you think he meant ambidextrous?'

'I suppose so, but what on earth did he mean by "*femme-homme*"?'

*   *   *   *   *

It is late afternoon. The red Fiat is back and we are driving through Manavgat again and over that unforgettable bridge which crosses the Melas.

'Let's see if we can find the mouth of the Melas,' I say.

We turn down a dirt road running parallel with the river.

'I hope you know what you're doing,' Duncan remarks.

'We shall soon see.'

The river disappears between banks of cane and tamarisk. The road becomes a sand-track winding through scrub and acres of stunted cotton. Already we are in a wilderness, and now from some dusty horizon a lorry-load of labourers looms towards us. Our own wheels churn into the sand like brown sugar and I am in terror of the car's stalling. A swarthy Turk in the lorry shouts at us to stop. His face is very like the face of the man in my dream who assaulted Duncan and left him dying: the same ruthless eyes, the same calculating leer. There is an instant of horror as our car shudders, but the wheels ultimately grip the sand and we shoot forward. Gradually the lorry lumbers into the distance. To Duncan I observe with nonchalance: 'We're not going to find any river-mouth. I'm ready to eat humble pie.'

'Thank God for that!' he says, and to myself I think: 'Oh yes, God, thank you. What if the car had stuck?'

Back once again in Manavgat we ask a group of men smoking and playing chess where the Falls of Selgas are. They direct us in a charade of signs and now we are headed out of the town towards the mountains. The elusive river no longer conceals itself but cuts an intermittent swathe of china-blue through the woods and cotton fields. Soon however we are in trouble again, for just as we come to the park where the Melas becomes the Falls of Selgas, the Fiat begins to hobble. We have a puncture.

Mechanically, Duncan is even more helpless than I am. I once had to show him how to use a tin-opener. He made a little sketch of it — appealingly *trompe-l'oeil* — and pinned it to the kitchen dresser in his flat at 24 Victoria Square. It remained there for years but he never succeeded in opening a tin.

To our relief a boy and his father approach us and before we know it they have the right tools out from the back of the car and are changing our wheel. I turn to Duncan.

'It's your venerableness, O Sage! Such venerableness in Turkey is a trump card.'

'I suppose you mean I give the impression of being a dithering old Methuselah on his last legs? And of course, you are right.'

'Don't be silly! You are young, and even children treat you as an equal.'

'Which means I'm on the same mental level.'

'Well, doesn't that please you? . . . Unless you become as little children you shall not enter into the kingdom of heaven.'

'That's a consolation!'

Now we are sitting under one of the giant plane trees, where rivulets of gin-clear water ripple between set-out tables. A few yards away, the River Melas throws up a mist of spray then hurls itself over a steep drop, and as it plunges shatters from chalk-blue into ice-white. Thence, from a tumbling pool it issues fresh and cerulean, sliding onwards between banks of terra-cotta and amber.

As we sip our rakis in the softening light, I ask Duncan about his early youth again.

'Tell me, were you considered a success at St Paul's School?'

'Well . . . I ask myself!'

'Your father had destined you for a career in the army?'

'That move had gone by. There *had* been an attempt to put me into the army class but it was obvious that none of my talents fitted there. Then I was put into the chemistry class and did no good there either.'

'Was there anything at school in which you were doing well?'

'I got prizes in the art school for painting and drawing, but my languages had gone to pot — I'd forgotten all my Greek — though I was interested in history and did some rather good essays which my master praised me for.'

'And why had your Greek — and presumably your Latin — gone to pot?'

'It was my being put into the army class and then into the chemistry class. There was simply no opportunity to continue my studies in language.'

'And so your academic career at this time — your eighteenth year — was really chaos?'

Duncan hesitates, searches for an answer, then breaks into laughter.

'It amounted to nothing. I was very bad at mathematics. I had no gift for anything except perhaps history.'

'And did this depress you?'

'No, not really. I used to pray every day that I could learn to paint like Burne-Jones . . . No, that came earlier . . . Then my Aunt Janie,* that wonderful woman, came to my rescue. She said to my father: "Look here, this boy is doing no good where he is, what he wants is to paint and to draw, let him go to an art school." '

'And so it was?'

'And so it was. I attended the Westminster School of Art for about two years, very much encouraged by Simon Bussy who was just then marrying Dorothy Strachey.'

'In much of your early life, while your parents were abroad, you lived with your Strachey cousins at Lancaster Gate. Was that a pleasant life?'

'It was an education. There was always something going on . . . seven lively and intelligent children, and a strong-minded tolerant aunt who encouraged us in every direction. There was play-writing and play-acting, music, dancing and games of every sort.'

'And who were some of your friends in London while you were a day-boy at St Paul's?'

'There was a family I used to go and have tea with on my way home: two brothers, Dick and Horace, and two sisters, Jane and Elly. I fell deeply in love with Elly and Horace. So obvious my love for Elly must have appeared that my mother asked me

---

* Lady Richard Strachey, Bartle Grant's sister.

one evening on going to bed whether I was very fond of her. "Yes," I said. I suppose it wasn't so obvious that I was deeply attached to Horace. When I told him so it came as a great surprise.'

'By the way, Duncan, be careful of these rakis. They've got a delayed-action kick . . . but go on.'

'Well, I used to flirt and laugh a good deal with our maid Lizzy, a delightful young woman who was willing to laugh and flirt innocently with me. One day my father came into the dining-room to find Lizzy perched on my knees and ragging. He obviously didn't think it quite as innocent as I did and hinted that it was enough . . . I received very little sexual education at this time of my life.'

'And so?'

'And so that's the end of that.'

As we listen to the steady purr of the Falls, my mind goes back to two unframed photographs propped on a studio dresser at Charleston of Duncan's father and mother – both in their early twenties, both stunningly beautiful – Bartle Grant and Ethel McNeil. Her romantic almost Pre-Raphaelite face is framed in black hair. He, in the uniform of a captain of the Guards, exudes a dashing masculinity which must have worked like a loadstone on the opposite sex. Ethel I met when she was in her nineties, and she looked about forty-five. Bartle died when Duncan was still a young man. In *The Memoirs of a Highland Lady*, written by Elizabeth Grant, Duncan's great-great aunt, there is a description of her young brother William: 'impractical, never out of humour, but quietly and thoroughly self-willed'. In the margin, scribbled in Bartle's own hand, are the words: 'Like me!'

Turning to Duncan again, I remark: 'You say that's the end of that, but tell me this: what were the relations of your father and mother when you were about sixteen? Were your parents still cohabiting?'

'You're asking me something I really don't know.'

'But your mother was having an affair with Commander Young, wasn't she?'

'That was already a going thing.'

'And your father had started his affairs?'

'Well, he was very . . . he was never very faithful.'

'Did your mother show any signs of resenting this?'

'Not to me . . . not to anybody.'

'Do you think she had to accept it?'

'I think *he* had to accept it.'

'He had to accept what?'

'Commander Young.'

'But didn't her affairs come after he'd begun his affairs?'

'Probably. I think she was quite happy with that: a much more important event in her life than my father's.'

70

'Because it was a real love affair?'

'Yes.'

'And your father's doings mere escapades?'

'I imagine so. Although one of his affairs, I think, was much more serious, with probably a child. He once took me to the opera with this old love of his and her son, who was just my age. And I always wondered if he was my father's son.'

'Did you get on with this putative half-brother of yours?'

'Oh yes! We went to see *HMS Pinafore* and both loved it.'

'Do you remember the woman's name?'

'Polly. She was called Polly.'

'Polly what?'

'I don't know. I remember Aunt Violet laughing with my father over a photograph of Polly as if it were a known thing, their affair.'

'The Victorians weren't as straitlaced as we think, were they?'

'Not in practice.'

'When your father expostulated with you about Lizzy sitting on your knee, he knew very well what *he* would be doing with her.'

'Certainly, and he presumed I would be doing the same.'

' "Father home from evensong sent for Cook and did her wrong"!'

'I never heard about *her*,' Duncan laughs.

It is dark. Rather unsteadily we load ourselves into the car, but when I press the starter nothing happens: a chortle, a stifled gurgle, and nothing. Oh lord, what if this had occurred in the wilderness! A man from the decrepit restaurant in the park hurries over, opens the bonnet and prods the engine with a wire. The Fiat gives out a roar and jerks into the night. There is no time even to thank him, and we are scudding along at a steady sixty towards Side. Duncan sinks into oblivion. I think of dinner. We press through the cricket-singing air when all of a sudden I find that we are cruising through pitch-darkness. The car lights have failed.

'What are we stopping for?' I hear Duncan dreamily murmur.

'We have no lights.'

'Why not?'

'Because they have gone out.'

'Oh God!'

September 26th

I have never been so loath to leave the table as I was last night at the Pamphylia when Ibrahim Cezir, the mechanic, came in half-way through my soup.

'How did you and your father ever get back?' he asked.

'We were given a lift.'

He looked incredulous and a little mortified.

'Where is the car now?'

'Stuck on the side of the road four kilometres from Side.'

'Come, we shall drive to the spot.'

I left Duncan sipping his soup. The red Fiat looked deader than ever on the lonely night road. Ibrahim and I pushed it further into the side. Today he is supposed to be dealing with it. Meanwhile, Duncan and I are back to our old way of living. He sketches, I explore. The choice of spot is always something of a wrangle. I insist on its being out of the sun, he insists on its being the right composition.

'Here's the perfect spot,' I say. 'And it'll be out of the sun for at least two hours.'

'A wretched composition,' he replies.

'But Duncan, it's lovely. Just look at the sea through those fig trees! If I were a painter I'd be transported.'

'You would be!'

This morning we have alighted again among the ruins overlooking the garden of the Hotel Pamphylia. This site should be good for several more mornings. Duncan sits in the shade of an ancient niched wall and sketches me in the nude as I face him in full sun. I read aloud from *Samson Agonistes*.

> O how comely it is and how reviving
> To the spirits of just men long oppressed
> When God into the hands of their deliverer
> Puts invincible might!

After a little, Duncan remarks: 'He's an even greater poet than I thought.'

'Perhaps, but there are times when he's downright longwinded. And he can spoil everything by his inversions. I think it's his sound that saves him. A schoolmaster once told me that his boys were having trouble with Milton. "Try reading him as if he didn't make any sense," I said. "Just keep the music of the line going. Roll out the glorious rhetoric as from an organ."'

'Did it work?'

'It did, once they'd lost their shyness, once they let the words pile up into a monument of chords.'

> . . .I dark in light exposed
> To daily fraud, contempt, abuse and wrong,
> Within doors or without, still as a fool,
> In power of others, never in my own;
> Scarce half I seem to live, dead more than half.

Peeping urchins, flabbergasted and agog with prurience, have forced me to don a g-string. Duncan's pastel sketch progresses, but I grow hotter and hotter. Occasionally I burst away into the sea, coming back by way of the pantry of the Pamphylia with a bottle of iced lager.

There is an interruption of another kind. Sirma Subutayi of the Genco Car Hire Service is on the line from Antalya.

'Our agent has seen the red Fiat,' she tells me, 'and has spoken to Ibrahim Cezir. The damage is serious. We've had to send all the way to Izmir for a new dynamo. It burnt out. You didn't turn the ignition key correctly. It will cost you 120 lira. No matter, you'll have the car in a couple of hours.'

'What nonsense!' I think. 'I turned the key the way it's designed to go: the way nine people out of ten would turn it.'

When I report to Duncan, he looks at me soothingly. 'We are in the hands of the Turks,' he says.

September 27th

Sirma Subutayi's 'couple of hours' has stretched. It does not bother us. Today, during the lull of the luncheon hour when the beach is deserted, Duncan has consented to embark on his second swim. He wears my white football shorts again and they sit on him with a Tweedledum compactness, though they do hang down rather – like Muslim drawers. With his straw hat still on his head he slowly walks into the sea.

'We'll stay at the edge this time,' I suggest, 'so you needn't be in the least nervous.'

'No indeed,' he replies with the utmost nervousness, 'and there's to be no attempt at swimming this time.'

We sit down together in the wash of small waves.

'Isn't it cooling!' I remark. 'Now lie down and you'll float.'

I put a hand under his back.

'Let your head rest on the water.'

I fling his hat onto the sands and Duncan, to his surprise, finds himself floating.

During lunch the conversation turns to Paris and painting again. I find I have been comparing him to Cézanne once more. Like Cézanne, the young Duncan Grant had to learn to control the exuberant romanticism of his temperament and the almost arrogant fertility of his imagination. Had I not seen him sacrifice canvas after canvas in the struggle to escape from mere virtuosity and so to arrive at the profounder truths? Yes, I was sure of it: to paint with the solidity of Chardin and the honesty of Cézanne was his life's training both as an artist and a humble man.

Duncan breaks into my reverie with: 'I find it rather shocking that we drink so much raki in the middle of the day.'

'That's your buried Scottish puritanism speaking,' I retort.

'Raymond Mortimer once said much the same. He was contrasting my early work with some of my later pictures, which he didn't like so much. "There's a strain of the puritanical Scot in you," he said.'

'I expect he meant you were trying too hard to tell the truth.'

'Something of that sort. He preferred my light-hearted early work.'

'Not for nothing were you once labelled "The Matisse of England"!'

'I believe the phrase was used . . . Anyway, Clive took Raymond to task in an article called "Festina Lente", reminding him that Monsieur Ingres too took some looking at. "Mr Mortimer is one of the most brilliant people I know," he wrote, "a delightful writer" and so on, "but he never looks more than a second at anything. He reads books at such a rate that they're finished before you can turn round; he shaves in a twinkling; and he does everything at such a pace that he can't be expected to look at pictures for more than a glance." '

'Didn't you sometimes find it bewildering, not to say disconcerting, to have so many experts telling you different things? There was Raymond wishing you'd go on being gay and fanciful, there was D.H. Lawrence deploring your experiments in abstraction, there was somebody else telling you to paint only abstracts, and heaven knows what Roger Fry and Clive were telling you.'

'I never took very much notice of what people said but kept to my instincts and to what I had learnt from painters like Piero della Francesca, Masaccio, Chardin, and of course Cézanne. And Simon Bussy's influence on me was always salutary.'

'What about Jacques-Emile Blanche?'

'A very intelligent man and a good teacher. It was Simon Bussy who recommended me to his school, "La Palette". Blanche encouraged me to do very careful drawings, and I think he was right. I was not at that time affected by the Post-Impressionists.'

'But you were by Chardin?'

'Yes. I used to go to the Louvre. I copied a Chardin there which I still have. Blanche used to take us round the Louvre on Sundays when it was closed to the public. He would pick out certain pictures and then describe them. Once he talked about the very painting I was copying and I didn't dare show him my copy . . . Silly!'

'All this came after you'd studied a couple of years at the Westminster School of Art?'

'Yes, in 1906 when I was twenty-one. An aunt of mine had left me £100 and I decided to go to Paris. The money had to last me the whole year.'

'You'd attended the Slade too?'

'Well, that came between my first and second period in Paris. I had two goes at the Slade, each time for a term or so. Tonks was the great man then. I remember during a life class saying to myself: "I know exactly what I must do to win approval here", and

I executed a drawing perfectly in the manner of Tonks. Sure enough, he took the bait. When he came round to me he held up my drawing as an example of what a good drawing should be. I felt rather mean, and also disillusioned.'

'But to get back to Paris . . . Were you on your own?'

'By no means. Two fellow students of mine at the Westminster School shared rooms with me: Ballard, the son of a left-wing politician, and Forestier – to whom I became very much attached – who was the son of a French illustrator in London. We all lived together near the Palais Royal in a hotel called Hôtel de l'Univers et du Portugal. It was kept by a very nice middle-aged old woman – an admirable person – who ran it impeccably. We had the cheapest rooms right at the top, a whole range of rooms, kept beautifully clean by Jacques, the servant who did out our rooms. There was no lift . . . We were happy there, and went to different schools.'

'Did you have any amorous adventures?'

'Well, there's the story of Forestier's uncle giving us both enough money to visit a brothel. The whole idea was good, very French and so often done for their sons. The uncle sent the money to Paris. There was a brothel just outside the door of our hotel. It had a red light and was a very well run brothel. Jacques used to keep an eye on the girls at the windows. He said he knew a good deal about the establishment. That led me to throw all to the winds and go there one evening.'

'With your friend Forestier?'

'No, that was the awful thing: alone. I was too shy to go with him. So I took my part of the money – 18 francs I think – and entered full of trepidation. Madame received me, surrounded by her girls. There was one extremely pretty one at the end, very young, and I simply went straight up to her and pointed. She and I were then taken upstairs by Madame.'

'And you acquitted yourself manfully?'

'Indeed I did. The girl was charming. She was new to the job and probably had just arrived from the country. She begged me to stay the whole night but I said I couldn't. No sooner had we begun to have another go when there was a tap at the door and time was up.'

'Was she crestfallen at your going?'

'She gave every appearance of being so. I promised I would come again if I could raise the money.'

September 28th

The red Fiat has finally reappeared, looking as dirty as ever. In my last parley with the Genco Car Hire Service I expressed our distrust of it. 'My father is nearly ninety,' I told them. 'What if it breaks down again, and in the wilderness?'

If I am right about the Turks' veneration for old age, this gambit will make something happen.

Tomorrow we plan to visit Aspendus, which is roughly half-way between Side and Antalya. The Roman theatre there, according to George Bean, is 'the best preserved ancient theatre of any kind anywhere in the world . . . built in the second century AD, perhaps under Marcus Aurelius'.*

We are still painting among the ruins overlooking the garden of the Pamphylia.

'Duncan, your interesting grandmother — your father's mother — did some pretty extraordinary things for a Victorian, didn't she?'

'Yes, she was a wonderful woman: really of an earlier age, not Victorian at all. She had the morals of a regency period.'

'Was it at Musoorie that she had her affair?'

'One of those hill stations . . . Juggerata . . . or it may have been Musoorie.'

'You said Musoorie before — my birthplace . . . It was during the hot weather, and with Lord Raglan, wasn't it?'

'Well, people say so, but I'm not so sure it wasn't Cardigan. And my grandfather was away being Governor of Madras . . . or perhaps Bengal . . . anyway, during the hot weather.'

'And she is up there flirting with Lord Raglan. Her husband comes back from the plains . . .'

'And discovers her with child.'

'And he forgives her?'

'Yes, he nobly forgives her. The result was Aunt Hennie. What's extraordinary is that the whole thing happened again the year after. My grandfather comes back from being Governor and finds her with child again.'

'By the same lover?'

'Yes. This time it's Uncle George.'

'And once more she's forgiven?'

'Yes . . . He couldn't very well have made a fuss.'

'Nevertheless, given the age, given their exalted position — a governor then was almost more than royalty — it's incredible.'

'Quite incredible. A wonderful story. My grandfather must have been a noble man. And my grandmother never lost the glint in her eye.'

'Do you remember your grandfather at all?'

'Only in the Doune at Rothiemurchus. I'd see him being wheeled about in a bathchair — quite stricken down. I don't think you could talk to him. He had a man servant who looked after him. My grandmother lived in a wing of her own . . . He just

---

* George Bean: *Turkey's Southern Shore*, Ernest Benn, 1968.

nodded to people he knew. He never spoke – not to me, anyhow.'

'He probably wondered if you stemmed from Lord Raglan.'

'I dare say.'

'Was he the laird of Rothiemurchus?'

'Yes, he came back from being Governor of Jamaica – after Madras – with very grand ideas and built up the Doune like anything, with lots of outhouses for masses of servants.'

'I'd like to see the Doune and discover the bedroom you were born in.'

'You'll find it in ruins.'

'What happened to Aunt Hennie and Uncle George?'

'They were brought up with the rest of the family. But they were very different. I never took to Uncle George. He had no charm. He became a distinguished civil servant and a clever man.'

'And Aunt Hennie?'

'She was dropped on her head as a child. Yes, from a cab in Rome. They were out driving and she was thrown out on her head. She behaved oddly for the rest of her life . . . She used to be sent out for long walks. Sometimes I went with her. We got on very well together. She and I were on the same intellectual level.'

September 29th

Once again I am at the wheel of the Fiat and we are speeding through the campagna towards Aspendus. Now, we turn off the main road and drive through an avenue of plane trees towards ochre hills. A wide river, the Eurymidon of antiquity, winds on our right through maize fields and orchards. I turn to Duncan.

'Do you realise this river was once navigable up to Aspendus itself, which is eight miles from the sea?'

'What else have you read up?'

'That at the mouth of the Eurymidon Xerxes and his Persians had a sea battle with the Athenians, who'd already defeated him at Salamis. Cimon, the Athenian admiral, wiped out his fleet. Then he dressed up his marines in Persian uniforms, put them on board captured Persian ships and landed them at night near the mouth of the river. The Persian camp was reduced to a shambles . . . All this happened just a few miles away.'

The massive seven-storeyed façade of the theatre now rears into view like an antique skyscraper.

'Duncan, what do you make of that?'

'I have no words for it.'

We get out of the car and walk slowly towards the beetling edifice. As we mount the stone steps, a dubious-looking youth with long sideburns – the kind that the villain always wore in old Hollywood movies – sidles up to me and hisses furtively: 'You want real ancient coins? I show you. I have special real ancient coins. Come.' Saying which he jingles something in his shirt pocket.

'Have nothing to do with him,' Duncan whispers. 'He has shifty eyes and I have no doubt he is a crook.'

'It's all right. I haven't the slightest interest in coins – except contemporary ones.'

'That too can be your undoing.'

I turn to the youth and say: 'Not now, thank you. Now we must see the theatre.'

Duncan walks with difficulty. His lumbago bothers him and he seems tired. He sits on some steps by the *skene* while I climb the enormous auditorium to the last tier. When I look down at him now, with a backdrop of three hundred feet rising behind him – a magnificent pile of columns and niches range on range, crowned by a triangular pediment showing Bacchus festooned with flowers – he seems pathetically dwarfed.

'Say something,' I shout. 'I want to hear what it sounds like from up here.' But he cannot make out what I am shouting. From an aperture in the great vault which supports the topmost rim of the theatre, I gaze out over fields and crops, fragments of aqueduct leapfrogging over the brown earth, and the opaque silver flash of the river. The *skene* is flanked by several storeys of dressing-rooms through which I wander. What productions, what excitement through the ages, have stemmed from these!

When I return to Duncan, he remarks: 'It's a sorrow to me not to climb all those steps with you. The size of the place is amazing.'

'I know, and it's still used for festivals and drama. George Bean says that on one recent occasion forty thousand people were crowded into the building. It was probably built to accommodate twenty thousand, but even this, when one considers that the Scala in Milan can barely manage five thousand, is incredible.'

'Why don't you mount the stage and recite something?'

'But there's no one in the auditorium to hear me.'

'Never mind that.'

I get up on to the *skene* and launch into the opening of the *Antigone* in Greek, but after six lines, which is all I have ever memorised, I notice someone standing listening in the middle tiers. He looks like a professor.

Now the coin-jingling youth is at my side again. He has latched on to me as I descend into the orchestra.

September 30th

All the way home from Aspendus yesterday I drove in a tumult of lament and rage; for, yes, I *did* succumb to the confidence trick of that hypnotic young man and parted with a great deal of money.

The professor said categorically that both the statuette and the coins I fell for were worthless. 'To me in the half-light of the shed he abducted me to,' I whimpered to Duncan, 'they looked so impressive.'

'I could have told you at first glance they were fraudulent and nasty,' he retorted. 'How could you have been such a ninny?'

'At least they'll make a nice necklace for someone,' I said.

'Yes, if you think having false coins round your neck is attractive.'

'But they say experience is cheap at any price.'

'If you can afford it. Which you can't.'

'Duncan, don't you see I'm crying out for a little comfort?'

'Then draw a curtain over the whole episode. Put it from you as though it had never been.'

'But how could I have done it? I'm not even interested in coins.'

'Fools and their money are soon parted.'

'Yes, I'm a fool. How can you love such a fool?'

'Especially a fool.'

This morning during breakfast, though it means leaving lovely derelict Side where we are safe and happy, we decide to look further afield. 'There is so much we haven't seen,' says Duncan.

We work out an itinerary which takes in Perge on the way to Antalya; and from there north-westwards along the coast for as far as the road will allow, we shall wander through the valleys of the Lycian range towards Phaselis: the Greco-Roman port where Alexander landed his troops on their march to the conquest of Persia. It is good to know, however, that we still have two days of Side.

Duncan is sitting under an awning of the restaurant where we dined last night off the square. It is open and breezy and he has chosen a composition of tables and chairs ranged across the restaurant in a vista towards the sea.

'That's rather a disconcerting subject,' I remark.

'I know. If anybody likes my pictures I don't want it to be because of the subject.'

'As you like! I'm going to explore the mouth of the River Melas.'

'What, not again?'

'You'll be all right here, and you can order your raki whenever you want.'

'Desertion, I see!'

'No – exercise and recreation.'

'Be off with you then.'

It is just after eleven and already I am some three miles from the ruins of Side, walking and running along the edges of the sea. I come upon a military encampment and creep past two tents with their opening to the shore. In each tent a soldier sits in unseeing bovine reverie. I slip on a shelf of rock just under the waves, grazing off a sliver of skin. Painful and annoying, but the salt and the sea will cleanse it. I am miles from anywhere and there is still no sign of the Melas. I must turn back, pass the enchanted backwater again with its plopping turtles, and browse through the cotton fields. It is after one o'clock when I walk into the square at Side.

Duncan is still painting under his awning.

'So you've started to celebrate,' I say.

'Yes, one must keep body and soul together . . . What have you found?'

'No river, but on my way back over what I'm sure is the old Roman road from Manavgat to Side, I came to an ancient cistern: probably where travellers watered their horses and washed the dust from their feet. You must see it. Two wide arches rise out of the sand, and the walls are niched for life-size statues. Two very old fig trees grip the drums of the toppled arches with labyrinthine roots: a wonderfully gnarled elephant-grey. I love the musty acridness of fig, don't you?'

'Yes, the very breath of the South.'

I stand behind him as he works. I see his problem. The vista across the tables has to take in not only the distance of the ocean but the closeness of the serried backs of chairs. To complicate matters, all the tables are now laid out with knives and forks and between these are patterns of bougainvillea petals sprinkled as if for a wedding.

He looks away for a moment. 'It's much too difficult.'

'Go on, you're doing splendidly. It looks like an abstract.'

'All good painting is abstract.'

'Is that something you learnt from Simon Bussy?'

'You mustn't pin me down. I've learnt it from everyone: from the mosaics at Ravenna, from the earlier designs and portraits of Greco-Roman art, from the early Italians . . . Yes, from them I learnt a lot about the boldness of design and how to relate figures and objects in space. Then in France there was Corot with his portraits and early landscapes, which taught me a great deal about how to balance the angle of one plane with another, and one movement with another.'

'Quite a litany! But what about England? I know you've copied Gainsborough and Constable.'

'Yes indeed, important influences! They taught me how to build up a composition steadily in small cumulative touches, balancing an upturn here with a downturn there: what Roger would call "compensating one movement and inclination with another". And from Constable I learnt a great deal about light out in the open.'

'I'm surprised you haven't mentioned Turner with all his colour. Some people think of you mainly as a colourist.'

'I can't help that. I go about things in a different way.'

'There's one way in which you and Turner *are* the same.'

'Oh?'

'He hogged his pictures and hated giving them up. He even bought them back. And yet he maltreated them – like you.'

'How can you say such a thing?'

'It's true. All your pictures at Charleston are carelessly stacked. They're scratched with nail marks because you refuse to hammer the nails into the stretchers properly, and for years you used a lovely flower piece to keep out the rain. Once I found a little sketch used as an oil rag. I straightened it out, found a frame for it, and sold it for good honest cash at Heals.'

'Who gave you permission?'

'You did – reluctantly.'

'Well, I must say, with such a glut of faults I wonder you have anything to do with me.'

'Because you are a colourist.'

Duncan laughs. I wish I had my camera with me. With his broad-brimmed hat shading his eyes and his brushes in one hand, he looks the epitome of an old master. Rembrandt's *A Man in a Cap* in the National Gallery could be his portrait. He rummages in his box of pastels as I attempt to explain.

'Yes, a colourist. Even at your most representational when, say, you have captured the solidity of a coffee-pot with all its plasticity and weight, you lay on your colours as if you weren't interested in verisimilitude but only in design. You keep your brush-strokes clear of one another as if they were notes in a symphonic scale, and the colours are pure and precise. You turn light into dark not by differences of tone, like the academics, but by differences of actual colour. You make illusions of dark by turning a shadow not from light green to darker green but from light green to a blue or a purple. And it works because these differences of colour share the right tones. What's more, when you want a landscape to recede, you don't do it by making the colours lighter: you change them.'

'My word, you *have* gone into things! I don't know what a wise man would say.'

October 1st

Tomorrow we leave Side, taking in the ruins of Perge on our way to Antalya. Our flight back to London, alas, is on the afternoon of the 7th from Istanbul.

Over our tea and grapes this morning, I ask: 'Do you like our existence here? Are you content?'

'Blissful, Don. Why can't it go on? No correspondence, no worries!'

'Why don't we stay another two weeks? I think we have the money.'

'No, my instinct tells me it would be a mistake.'

'I won't press your instinct.'

I have driven into Manavgat, leaving Duncan to finish his sketch under the restaurant awning. We shall need a lot of cash. There will be the bill at the Pamphylia for dinners, beers, rakis and bottles of wine. And there is still that fraudulent account to settle for the broken Fiat.

Driving past the old palaces and aqueducts, the olives and warm sepia-tinted fields, I reflect on our conversation at breakfast. Yes, it is true: we lead an uncluttered life – no newspapers, no post, no people to see. We live like children, sunk in the experience of each moment. Duncan's devotion to painting sometimes makes me feel that I am leading a lazy life, dedicated to nothing but lying in the sun, but all this antiquity soaking through me will, surely, work its magic.

It is lunchtime when I arrive back at the square in Side. The place has filled up with desultory Sidetans sitting outside the cafés with youths and maidens (mostly German and American) resting heavy knapsacks on the flagstones, and tourists pouring out of charabancs. Duncan is putting a last touch or two to his sketch of tables and chairs looking towards the sea.

'You're so assiduous,' I comment. 'Where did you learn such single-mindedness?'

'I early got the habit of work. One day in Paris it came to me very forcibly that I must make a choice. Either I could go in for a good time or I could be a serious painter. I chose.'

'Not that you haven't had a good time!'

'No, but I always put painting first.'

'And you're a mystic.'

'Oh!'

'Well, at least you had two mystic experiences. There was that one at Streatley-on-Thames where you were staying with your parents. And you heard a voice.'

'I did, loud and clear – like a command. I was about eighteen and I was painting a landscape. "You must go out into the world," it said, "and learn all there is to know, and be seen in the world of painting. And there are other things going on at this very moment about which you know nothing." '

'And you obeyed?'

'Who was I to say "nay" to deity!'

'Tell me about that other occasion when you saw Christ.'

'Yes, I saw Christ coming up the aisle when I was confirmed by the bishop. He stopped and laid his hand on me.'

'Then what?'

'Later I told James Strachey.'

'And the clever Strachey took your faith away!'

'Well, "Let's look up Christianity in the *Encyclopaedia Britannica*," he said. So we looked it up together and he read it out. Then he turned to me and said: "Do you mean to say you believe all this?" The effect was instantaneous. My Christianity fell away from me like a mantle.'

'Oh, the serpent!'

October 2nd

Yesterday, during Duncan's siesta and in spite of my fiasco with the coins, I could not resist putting in some surreptitious buying. In the entrance hall of the Pamphylia stands a cabinet displaying antique rings, terra-cotta figurines and jewellery. There was a ring there which attracted me from the first, and a Byzantine pendant cross. The question was, how to pay for them.

'*Patron*,' I said, after I had settled our bill, 'I notice you have a passion for gadgets. I've seen you fiddling with all that snorkel stuff. And the other day you doted over a transistor radio . . . How much do you want for that ring and the pendant?'

He was in his bathing trunks as usual and languidly answered: 'I'll let them go for a thousand. I'd ask two from anybody else. The ring is a genuine piece, made by hand; so is the cross . . . Do you have a tape-recorder?'

'I do, but it's too useful to me to part with. What about an electric shaver? It's a Ronson and in mint condition.'

'Let me see it.'

Feeling like a thief I tiptoed past the snoring Duncan and fetched the shaver from our room. The *patron* examined it.

'Add 500 lira and it's a deal,' he said.

I was elated. The ring with its coral-coloured cornelian was already on my finger. The pendant cross would be a suitable present for Clarissa, my wife.

In the evening we drove over a dirt road to the ruined cistern I discovered the day before. The sun, low over the Aegean, slanted across forum, theatre and sand-dune; the whole place was brushed with gold. Duncan sketched the arch rising out of the massive drum of Roman brick. I let the shadow of my body fall into one of the niches so that it looked like a fresco in charcoal, and after some manoeuvring managed to photograph this. The roots of the wild fig crawled over the base of the pillar with adamantine grip.

'Duncan, wouldn't Edward* have loved this?'

'He would have, and he'd certainly have come to Turkey with us.'

'Edward should never have died when he did.'

'No indeed, life has never been quite the same.'

I could not help smiling when I thought of the invariable pattern of Duncan's

---

* Edward le Bas, RA. One of Duncan's younger painter friends, they met over the signing of one of Duncan's pictures.

meetings with Edward le Bas. Hardly would he arrive at Victoria Square from the country when he telephoned Edward and their discussion of plans was always the same.

'Edward, my dear, we can't possibly accept another invitation from you to dinner. You must come to us.'

'Very nice of you, but I do happen to have two plump capons . . . and there's a Camembert which reached perfection yesterday, and it'll only be ruined if you and Don don't come here.'

Duncan continued my thoughts unawares: 'What a host he was, and what a friend!'

It was dark when we left and we drove to the Pamphylia for our last dinner in Side.

It is mid-morning and we are cruising at a comfortable eighty towards Perge. The breeze flows through the car and makes us forget how hot the weather has become. I am full of confidence because the car is no longer the dirty red Fiat but a sparkling white one.

'Duncan, your venerableness has scored again. Even the Genco Car Hire Service has made its obeisance.'

'It's the least they could do.'

The car is loaded with all our chattels: Duncan's blue canvas bag bulging, my battered black one, the ubiquitous basket with its pot-pourri of the things he likes to have on tap – passport, handkerchief, purse, cigarettes, sunglasses, clock. In it too are our cognac, vodka, raki and wine.

'Duncan, how well did you know George Mallory, who disappeared on Mount Everest?'

'Very well indeed. I did lots of paintings of him, but they all seem to have disappeared.'

'There's that sitting nude which belongs to Rex Nan Kivell. It's very fine.'

'They were mostly nudes. He was a beautiful creature and was perfectly willing to sit to me naked.'

'He probably liked being admired.'

'Yes, that was obvious.'

'Was he narcissistic?'

'No, I don't think so . . . I met him first at Cambridge through Lytton. The last time I met him in the nude was very suitable: on the eve of his marriage. We had dinner together in his rooms at Charterhouse School, where he was a housemaster. He was innocent and gay. A most engaging character.'

We have arrived outside the enormous gates of Perge and as we get out of the car the heat hits us like a whiff from a furnace. Duncan staggers towards a chair in the shade of a palm-thatched kiosk. He says his back and thighs are hurting. I order beers and he swallows two Anadin tablets with his. Now, very haltingly, we move into the ruined city, where he sits on a stone in the refuge of a shadow while I set off down the magnificent colonnaded street.

As I walk, I cannot help thinking of St Paul and St Barnabas walking down these same arcaded streets in all their glory. It was the height of the Roman period and luxurious shops must have made it something like a Burlington Arcade . . . except that it was twice as broad with a runnel of water six feet wide flowing down the middle. The two apostles landed at Perge after their voyage from Cyprus, 'passing through', the Acts say, on their way to Antioch. Not long after, they were in the city again and St Paul preached there.

In those days one could sail seven miles up the River Cestrus (now the Axu) to within a short distance of Perge itself: impossible to believe if one catches a glimpse of the undistinguished stream which pokes its way through cotton fields and scrub. It was in 333 BC that the young Alexander wintered his Macedonians at Phaselis, then marched on Perge. The city offered no resistance and he made it his headquarters.

Coming back to Duncan I find him still sitting in the shade of the outer gate.

'You may be sitting in the very spot St Paul sat in,' I tell him.

'Maybe, but with a very different mind.'

'Yes, an unregenerate mind.'

'I think that's going rather far . . . but I see what you mean.'

I walk with him to the great round towers of the inner gate so that he can see the beginning of the colonnaded street, and I help him to sit on a fallen pedestal.

'Would you like a little bit of guidebook now?'

'Certainly.'

'All right. Artemis of Perge was the great goddess here. Her title on the earliest Pamphylian coins was "Vanassa Preiia" or Pergean Queen. I wonder if that's where Swift got the name of Vanessa for his heroine? It must mean "queen" . . . Or was Vanessa really the anagram for his mistress, Esther van Homerick? Anyway, a battery of priests and priestesses kept her cult going, not only at Perge (which seems to have been her "Mecca") but at shrines throughout Asia Minor.'

'Oh yes, Diana of the Ephesians,' Duncan murmurs.

'Who got St Paul so worked up . . . Or was it the other way round?'

'You mustn't ask *me*.'

'Anyway, the guidebook says Vanassa was something of an Asiatic goddess and in her simplest form was represented by a rectangular block of stone surmounted by a female bust. According to George Bean it may have been a meteoric block fallen from the skies which the Greeks identified later with their own Artemis. Be that as it may, Perge waxed fat on the offerings of the devout. So fat that the notorious Verres could not keep his hands off her . . . Do you remember about Verres, Duncan? Cicero's great diatribe against him was one of my books at school.'

'I can't say I do.'

'Well, he was a Roman magistrate who in 80 BC became a legate on the staff of Dolabella, Governor of Cilicia. They were both crooks and proceeded to rob, bleed and plunder the province with such blatancy that, even for a Roman governor, it became a scandal. Dolabella was recalled, stood trial in Rome and was convicted. Verres saved himself by giving evidence against his boss. You'd think he would have learnt his lesson. Far from it. Through massive bribes he got himself made Governor of Sicily, the richest province in the Roman Empire. In four years he reduced the economy of that prosperous state to a shambles. When he returned to Rome Cicero launched into him in one of the most famous trials in history. Verres, with all his money, hired Hortensius, the best lawyer in Rome, to defend him. Cicero's opening speech was so devastating that Hortensius refused to reply and advised his client to leave the country.'

'Was that the last of him?'

'Cicero in a series of terrific speeches tore him to pieces. Verres went off and lived in Marseilles and was eventually proscribed by Mark Anthony.'

'Extraordinary and fascinating!'

While Duncan is musing on these things, I take some photographs. After ten minutes I am back and hand the camera to him. 'Duncan, I want to be in some pictures. Pull yourself together.' There ensues the following scene.

'Where do I stand?'

'Exactly on this spot. You have nothing to do but look through this little hole – no, this one, where my finger is – and press the trigger . . . the trigger, yes, where this other finger is.'

I then retreat to my position and compose myself. But bafflement no. 1 is on Duncan's face. He holds the camera a foot away from himself and is trying to gaze through the film-replacement socket.

'No no, not that hole . . . the one on the top left-hand corner.'

Hesitation and fumbling follow. He turns the camera in every direction but not in mine. I step out of my pose with a groan.

'See this opening? Well, glue your eye to it.'

I return to my position. A bird flies overhead, a car passes in the distance, a butterfly settles on a stone, but from Duncan – nothing. Now he is pointing the camera at his feet and bafflement no. 2 is on his face.

'I can see nothing,' he says.

'Oh, Duncan, you're not aiming at me and your finger's right over the lens. Of course you can't see anything.'

With a hurt look he removes his finger.

'Can you see me now?'

'Yes.'

86

'Am I all in?'

'Y-yes.'

'Are you sure?'

'That depends. The top of your head isn't seen.'

'But I've given you the exact position to get me all in: head to toe.'

'Oh.'

'Am I in now?'

'Yes, you're all in now.'

Half a minute passes. My epic pose is decomposing. 'For God's sake press the trigger.'

Still nothing. The relaxed half-smile I have cozened my face into turns into a slit-eyed, disagreeable glare as I see Duncan pressing one part of the camera after the other. 'The trigger, Duncan, the trigger! I put your finger right on it . . . You're not a Neanderthal man are you?'

(Meek and lost) 'Yes.'

Back in my place and far from ready to say 'Now,' I am struggling to salvage from my features some look of not utter impatience, when I hear a click.

Lingering by the Great Gate and sitting in the shade on cool slabs of fallen marble, we continue to talk as I read intermittently from the guidebook.

'Perge must have been a city flowing with waters,' I remark, 'full of baths, cisterns, fountains.'

'Like Rome,' Duncan adds.

'One day I'm going to come back here,' I say, 'and be more thorough. I'll climb the acropolis, where the citizens used to retire when the city was attacked.'

I see a wistful look pass over Duncan's face and he murmurs: 'I shall not be there.'

'Oh Duncan, you'll always be here in my memory.' I quickly pass on: 'I wonder if by then anyone will have solved the mystery of the famous temple of Artemis. D'you know, in spite of all its richness and fame, not a trace of it has been found.'

Now we are back in the car, driving past the vaulted arches of the stadium on our way to the theatre: a building converted from Greek to Roman in AD 100. This was thirty-three years after Perge had become Roman and begun her greatest period of prosperity. As at Aspendus, the stage building is several storeys high, the façade embellished with pillars, pediments, friezes and niches. A mass of fallen blocks littering the orchestra have recently been cleared, but more are crowded into the *skene* itself, all waiting to be placed. I have seated Duncan in the shadows of a vault through which a current of cool air flows. There is nobody about but a vendor of postcards sitting under the vault of the parados.

'We don't want any postcards, do we, Duncan?'

'Not unless you can find something irresistible.'

I have a quick look through and alight on a reproduction of one of the panels of the fallen frieze: Apollo driving in triumph in a small chariot drawn by two lionesses.

'Here's something irresistible.' I show it to Duncan.

'Yes, it's superb. Buy me some too.'

Just after one o'clock we drive into Antalya. I make straight for the Hotel Perge, where we were comfortable and content two weeks ago. The clerk shakes his head. They are full up. So I leave Duncan in an armchair and take myself to the Pension Nuri, two hundred yards down the street. A young man shows me a spacious room on the ground floor overlooking an orchard of tangerines. Under the tangerines a few long-legged chickens scrabble and wander. The heavy cavernous shade of the room is a delicious contrast to the glare outside. 'Yes, we'll take it for one night,' I tell him.

We pass out for hours in the shuttered coolness of that room at the Nuri. Then we dine at our favourite restaurant, the Sherik. It buzzes with people as before, the waiters are as efficient as ever, and the variety of unknown dishes as tempting as ever.

'All I want is a soup and a salad,' Duncan says.

'*I* want very much more. There's a magnificent fish behind a glass – two feet long . . .'

'You deserve it.'

The giant fish came. I assaulted it like a Lucullus and left only a backbone skeleton worthy of the Natural History Museum in South Kensington.

'Duncan, the other day in an art gallery off Bond Street a young man introduced himself to me by the name of Hobhouse. He was fair, an English Greek god type, and said that his grandfather had been a very great friend of yours.'

'Yes, indeed, Arthur Hobhouse. I met him through Maynard and Lytton at Cambridge. He *was* a Greek god.'

'Did you have fun and games with him?'

'Not then.'

'Was he attracted to you?'

'He must have been, up to a point, because he didn't resent what you call "fun and games". I arranged to go to the Orkney Islands with him and Maynard for a summer holiday and on the way we passed through Rothiemurchus where he caused a sensation among the ladies.'

'At the Doune?'

'Yes. I heard one of the young maids call out to Myra the cook: "Oh, there's the most beautiful young man you've ever seen," and I thought she meant me.'

'Did you like him?'

'Yes, a lot. He didn't say very much, but he wasn't stupid . . . Well, we were all in the Orkneys together for a time. While I painted, Maynard was busy on his book *Economic Consequences of the Peace*.'

Hayfield, 1953, collection of the author

Poppies, c. 1955, collection of the author

'Were you and Maynard having an affair?'

'Yes, more or less.'

'Why, more or less?'

'Because I don't think that was the peak of our relationship. Then Arthur and I were lent a remote house on the estate with a guest-room for two. That's when I really got to know him.'

'So you were having a double affair?'

'If you like, though Maynard must have gone home . . . My association with Hobhouse only lasted about a year and a half. It came to an end by his sudden wish, in a house just off Bond Street where he was living with his family. He was desperate to keep his mother ignorant of our affair, but my passionate remonstrations and expressions of despair must have reached the butler's ears. Anyway, Hobhouse told me not to visit him again.'

'Did you want to?'

'Yes – I hardly gave it a thought – but he was terrified of being found out. His decision was sprung upon me.'

'Did you see him again after that?'

'Casually.'

'Did he remain beautiful?'

'Yes. He lived to about eighty. He brought his wife once to see me at Gordon Square as an act of friendship . . . She, I dare say, had had to be told about it.'

'What, the affair?'

'Yes.'

'Wasn't that unnecessary?'

'It was, but he was full of unnecessary duties. That was part of his troubles.'

'Did you like his wife?'

'I hardly spoke to her. Though she was very kind. It was just a social call . . . about a year or so after our parting.'

October 3rd

The bill for the fish last night seemed to me a little steep, at least for the modest Sherik – £2. It shows how scarce fish have become in the Mediterranean. The *patron* at the Pamphylia told us that there is almost nothing left in the waters around Side. And yet, only a few years ago the coast of Southern Turkey was famous for the variety, quantity and excellence of its fish.

Now we are in the car again and heading for the coast road under the Lycian mountains. Our one night at the Pension Nuri was the noisiest we have spent in Turkey except for the first: not because of the music coming from the cafés in the park, but because of those same long-legged game-fowls I had seen strutting under the tangerine trees – I mean the cocks. From midnight onwards they, and others they stimulated on terraces and verandas throughout Antalya, proclaimed false dawns. I had always been led to believe that one could trust a cock. Like dogs and children they were supposed to have their fingers – paws, talons – on the pulse of truth. Not so. Like dogs and children they are great liars. They profess what it profits them to profess, and they believe what they dare not disbelieve. Duncan, however, slept through the whole cockerel performance and when I told him what I thought, he said: 'I don't think it's true that children are great liars. It's simply that they don't have the words to express the truth, so they invent things.'

'Be that as it may,' I answered, 'nobody's going to tell me the cocks of Antalya aren't masters of the lie.'

Our road has begun to climb into cliffs of russet rock fringed with pine trees. The bay of Antalya seems a long way away and its ring of new high-rise flats look like dolls' houses. Now the road swings down again, dipping into an exquisite enclave of the sea, sand and trees. The scenery is beginning to remind me of the Costa Brava when I first discovered it: a coastline of mountains, bays and virgin inlets.

'Look, Duncan, we're going up again . . . Good heavens! The road here is still being laid.'

I have to slow down to ten miles an hour as we grind over rubble and broken stone. We are on a brand-new road that is only a quarter finished. And the sea is now a long way beneath us: a sheer drop of hundreds of feet. A loaded lorry swings round the corner towards us. It neither leaves us room nor slackens pace. I stop dead, hoping it will just clear us. Smack! It has caught us on the left mudguard and is blithely careering on.

'Incredible!' I shout. 'It could have knocked us into the sea or squashed us into the mountain . . . The absolute brute!'

'What a good thing you stopped!'

'I should have rushed out and taken his number. There's no point in chasing him. I don't want to be knifed.'

'I should think not.'

Our left rear-light is smashed and there is a hefty dent in the car. We continue somewhat sobered. The 'road' now is nothing but an elevated shelf of rocks and pot-holes and we are down to walking pace.

'We've come so far now, Duncan, it would be even worse to turn back, even if we *could* turn on this trapeze.'

I marvel at his sang-froid. Duncan is on the edge seat, almost hanging over the precipice, and yet he sits there as though we were in a traffic jam in Fleet Street and he is admiring St Paul's.

'I shouldn't mind a pee,' he says.

'Oh, Duncan, for once you'll have to pee in your pants.'

'I may take you at your word.'

At last the road descends. There seems to be nothing but plain now, stretching endlessly between sea and mountains. We come to a palm-thatched shelter with the legend 'Café' stuck up on a post. It could have been 'Ben Gun was once here'. It is time for lunch.

'Perhaps we can get our *oeufs-sur-le-plat*,' Duncan says.

'And you can have your pee.'

'I don't want it any more.'

'Well, at least we can have a beer.'

A man appears, with the lugubrious look of an unshaven Byzantine Christ. He neither welcomes us nor turns us away. No, there are no *oeufs*. As if I doubted him, he opens the door of a small refrigerator: empty of food but full of bottles of beer. Without veering from his gloomy look he opens two bottles and brings them to us under the palm thatch. Then, to our amazement, he puts a chair within two feet of us, sits down, and gazes.

I turn to Duncan. 'Is he, do you think, extending to us the utmost in Turkish hospitality? Is it rude in Turkey to stop staring?'

'More likely, he's watching us to see we don't help ourselves to another beer.'

'Certainly he'd knife us without batting an eyelid.'

'Charm is not his strong point,' Duncan adds.

All this we speak right to his face, smiling all the time to show we hold him in highest regard.

I walk along the edge of the sea, longing to fling off everything and lie in the sun. But this is the wrong place for idyllic lingering. The eyes of the Turk are on us.

The long straight road between mountain and shore is punishingly sharp and pitted. Sometimes it climbs and turns, to reveal yet another pine-sheltered bay. Sometimes the woods give way to fields of cotton and maize, and sometimes we cross shingly river-beds guarded by colonies of enormous rocks. So long as we keep moving, Duncan finds the heat bearable, but I am apprehensive of breaking down in this beautiful wilderness and dare not drive faster than fifteen miles an hour.

'Ah, *finalmente*!' I am able to burst out at about two. 'Those are orchards of orange, pomegranate and mulberry. And I see a farmhouse. We're coming to something.'

Within a mile or two we find ourselves in the centre of a village. It is Kemer. A group of men and youths, propped up within the shade of a large plane tree, eye us curiously. Some sit at tables.

'Is there a restaurant?' I ask.

A man in an apron comes forward and directs us to a low white house under another plane tree. It is his restaurant. The man helps Duncan out of the car with all the reverence due to a patriarch and practically carries him to a chair beneath the tree. I go to inspect the kitchen. Apart from a few pots there is no sign that a meal has ever been prepared in the place. Nor is there any sign of cook, waiter or fire.

'Could we have fried eggs?'

'Oh yes, immediately.'

'And a bottle of red wine?'

'Of course.'

I myself begin to lay the table under the plane tree. Our host is eager and quick. It seems less than five minutes before we are actually eating. He too takes a chair and sits smiling and watching.

'Do you want a room for the night?' he asks.

'Perhaps,' I reply warily; then I whisper to Duncan: 'Let's not commit ourselves. I've a feeling we can do better.'

'But we'll mortally offend him if we don't accept his place. Just look at him!'

'In that case we'll present him with a *fait accompli*. Just before we entered the village did you notice a large house and a garden, and people finishing their lunch under cane-covered pergolas? Well, my instinct is to try there first . . . I'll be back in twenty minutes.'

Leaving Duncan sipping coffee under the benign stare of our host, I am soon conversing with a gentle-faced stripling who speaks to me in Italian. He leads me through an avenue of orange trees towards a long two-storeyed building still being built. All around it are bricks, tiles, bags of cement and a concrete mixer. 'My father, my brother and I are building this guest-house,' the young man says. Then he unlocks a door and we enter a bedroom of sparkling whiteness. The simple furniture looks handmade. The curtains, the two beds, the cupboard built into the wall – everything is new and everything tasteful. A wooden-framed window opens on to the orange grove and across to the sea.

'This will do us admirably,' I say.

'*Demi-pension* is 75 lira.'

'Is that for two? I have my *bapu* with me.'

'Yes, for both of you.'

'All we want in the morning is a big bowl of *caffè-latte*. We might occasionally need a packed alfresco luncheon, and always dinner in the evening.'

'All that is easy.'

I have rejoined Duncan under the plane tree. Nearby, a little stream flanked by yellow canna runs in front of the restaurant. Glancing into it I see a terrapin the size of a demitasse saucer disappear under a leaf. I put my hand into the water and fetch him out, all olivine and glistening – 'Look, Duncan!' – then return him to his cool haunt.

Somewhat sadly our *patron* shakes hands with us as we get back into the car. 'Are you staying in the hotel?' he asks. 'Yes,' I say. Nothing more.

92

Duncan has tossed himself down between the sheets of his clean new bed like one staggering in from the Sahara. The room is as cool as the inside of an Italian church in August. Meanwhile, I delay my own siesta and drive the car on to a sandy arm of the bay.

On my left is a small hilly peninsula of warm rose-coloured rocks tufted with pines and aromatic shrubs. On the opposite cliff across the gulf, a spur of trees runs down to the sea and on the higher ground merges into the mysterious dips and clefts of Mount Climax. The bay is of exquisite remoteness, and yet, rising right in the middle of it like a new Jerusalem is a miniature city: a florescence of white turrets, facets and windows which sparkle on the bosom of the dark wild hill like a cluster of jewels on the skin of a gypsy. I have never seen a more beautiful marriage of art and nature.

Back in our little room, Duncan and I sit on our beds and look out into the growing delicacy of the light.

'You must come and see what I discovered this afternoon,' I tell him. We drive out to the promontory and gaze at the townlet in the bay. The crags behind are turning to amethyst.

'I must sketch this tomorrow,' he says.

We attempt to question two men walking along the road about this extraordinary piece of architecture, but all I can get out of them is that it was built by Italians.

* * * * *

'Duncan, would you have fought in the last war if you'd been the right age?'

'Certainly. I think it was very different from the First World War, which was more about stupidity on both sides than against evil.'

'Do you look back with any bitterness on all those years you had to put in as a farm labourer, I mean from 1916 onwards?'

'Not at all, though I was often too exhausted to paint. But I liked being in the country. Besides, Vanessa, Bunny Garnett and I had only just moved into Charleston and there was plenty to distract us.'

'I love the story of Lytton Strachey before the pacifist tribunal when his case came up.'

'It's very well known.'

'But tell me again.'

'Well, we all went to support him with our testimonies. Lytton cut rather a figure of fun from the beginning and proceeded to blow up a rubber cushion to sit on. When the judge turned to him and said: "And now, Mr Strachey, what would you do if a fine strapping Hun attempted to rape your sister?", Lytton replied: "In such an eventuality, m'Lord, I should endeavour to put my own body in between."'

* * * * *

93

At dinner under the pergolas we are given ample opportunity to observe the family. There are five of them. Papa and two sons are not only building the annexe Duncan and I are housed in but help to run the guest-house. Mama and a beautiful daughter cook, cater and serve. They all appear to be fluent in German.

'Smart of them!' I remark, 'for there seem to be more Germans in Turkey than any other foreigners.'

'Like Italy,' he answers.

Indeed, there are two tablefuls of young Germans preparing to eat.

'England has missed the bus in Turkey,' I comment. 'She seems quite willing to let Germany run it. Is that a gross generalisation?'

'Not here it seems . . . The Germans have always yearned for a place on the Mediterranean.'

'Did you know that these pressure lamps are made in Germany?'

'No.'

'It's stamped on the lamp in our room.'

The *patron* is now lighting and hanging up the lamps. They have bulbous bases like flattened footballs and shed their light through a mantle. They glow with a fierce luminosity, as bright as a hundred-watt bulb and yet somehow softer.

The *patron* is a greying but vigorous man of about fifty, five foot ten or so. He has the kindliest eyes. He does not seem to give orders and yet his authority is everywhere. His manners are full of thoughtfulness. When Duncan arrives or departs — as we are soon to find — he puts down whatever he is doing and comes to take his arm. Like all the family, he is indefatigable: mending equipment on a table strewn with tools, looking after his guests, measuring terraces for the new annexe. His elder son — the boy who converses with me in Italian — is distinguished by the same air of gentleness. He is a well made youth, amply and roundly fleshed, with an oval face which reflects intelligence but no guile.

I say to Duncan: 'He reminds me of a fifth-century-BC statue of Bacchus — the same smoothly muscled torso, its strength hidden by softness of contour.'

'He's as thoughtful as his father,' Duncan comments.

'I know. Last night he escorted me with a torch through the orange grove, and this morning he insisted on carrying our breakfast all the way from the kitchen although I'd gone myself to fetch it. Because of his Italian he's our sole source of information. I've asked him about the possibility of going by boat to Phaselis.'

'Where's that?'

'A few miles up the coast north of Kemer. It's an old Roman port. Bacchus says he can arrange it for tomorrow. Would you like to go?'

'By all means.'

'Incidentally, there's one thing about Bacchus I'm surprised you haven't noticed.'

'Oh.'

'Well, you see his astonishing disregard of dress . . . one minute he's washing dishes and the next mixing cement, so he doesn't mind what he looks like, but in a certain item he has carried his nonchalance to an extreme. The zip of his khaki shorts is broken and they're also torn. Quite often you can see everything.'

'That's his innocence.'

'I know but isn't it a curious thing that we're conditioned to see only what we expect to see? I don't think a single person here has noticed this undraped aspect of his godhead.'

'One might have thought his mother and his sister would.'

'They're too busy in the kitchen . . . what do you think of Madame's cooking?'

'It's really rather good. She looks to me like an intelligent woman.'

'Yes, I have a feeling she could easily sit down and discuss Goethe or Hölderlin with us if only we could speak German . . . what about Bacchus's brother? He's about four years younger.'

'He doesn't have his charm. He looks sweet but rather thick.'

October 4th

It is about nine and as I draw the curtains a lively sun floods on to our beds. 'Duncan, we're going for a sea voyage.' He grunts from under his sheet, and I say: 'Have you nothing more brilliant to say than that?'

He sits up with a mischievous look: 'I leave brilliance to others.'

I walk through the orange grove to see about our breakfast. Madame understands what we want: no, no bread and jam, just a large bowl each of *caffè-latte*. While this is being prepared I am able to watch the beautiful girl. She must be about nineteen: neither tall nor short, with a classic face of perfect symmetry. Her eyes and hair are black. Though the colouring is quite different, she reminds me of my own Pandora, who is the same age and studying at the Ruskin School of Fine Art. They share something of the same stillness, the same paradoxical illusion of aloofness yet concern. How hot do you want the milk, sir? Are you sure you would not like bread, butter and jam? I like her unobtrusive objectivity.

We have had breakfast and I am backing the car. There is a crash and a tinkle. I have run into the wheelbarrow. Its iron handles have gone through the rear light which the rogue lorry spared. The ground is strewn with red glass. Those are squiggles of wire that once were lights. With its dent in the side the white Fiat is now a flawed thing. Like a true Libran I have lost all affection for it.

Our two skippers inform us they are prepared to spend the whole day at Phaselis for the sum of 100 lira, about £3. A bargain! Leaving Duncan sitting on pine needles and sketching the bay, I drive back to Madame's kitchen to collect an alfresco lunch. She has put together half a large loaf, four giant tomatoes, a hunk of feta cheese, a melon and a bottle of wine.

Our vessel is one of those small sturdy boats which are much the same from Genoa to the Bosporus: inevitably powered by a rickety, smelly diesel engine that drowns conversation. Our boat is just small enough to be handled by oars if the need arises. We were ushered on board like royalty and are now phut-phutting across the bay, the clumsiness of our power a contrast to the slipping of the bows over the limpid depths. Once round the promontory we glide beneath tiers of honey-coloured cliff, as rich as layer-cake and topped by a fringe of shrubs. The sea and the sky are incredibly blue and the breeze off the land is fragrant. Now the cliffs are giving way to leagues of plain merging into long stretches of warm empty beach. Behind all this the mountains lend such solitude that one cannot help thinking no foot has trod here before. The rocking of the boat and the drumming of the engine is an incantation. Already Duncan has succumbed to the spell and is measured out along the starboard gunwales, his head propped on a pile of fishing gear. I cover him against the sun, and then in my g-string stretch out myself on the poop deck. With thoughts of Homer, and all the civilisations that have risen and fallen in this cradle of the Mediterranean, I fall asleep.

An hour must have passed. I awake to see the helmsman gazing at Duncan and me in turn. He is a solid, pleasant-faced man just past middle age. Gesturing and mouthing over the throb of the diesel he asks how old Duncan is. I hold up the fingers of both hands nine times. A look of incredulity comes over his features and he beckons to his companion. They gaze at *me* now and I feel myself caught in a dilemma. If I tell them my age it will be embarrassing: the flower of youth in the East fades so fast. So I lie. Even so I fail to make myself young enough. A sad sober consternation comes into their faces, as if to say: '*We* are old men. The youth of these two puts us to shame. What is their secret?'

The engine cuts out and we glide into the middle bay of Phaselis. It is ringed with pine trees merging into a thick wood. The bay on our right is backed by an escarpment of rust-coloured rock. White ruins tumble along the shore into the sea. The bay on our left is invisible through a scrub of conifers and myrtle.

I find the moment exciting as I jump calf-deep into the water. Our boat has ground on to the sandy bottom. Now the two skippers lower Duncan on to my shoulders and like Aeneas carrying Anchises from burning Troy (but with none of his monumental assurance) I stagger with him up the shingly slope.

'*That's* a relief!' he says, as I lower him into a pool of pine shade.

'Yes, and here's a glass of wine! . . . I've given our sailors half our loaf and half the melon. They're ecstatic and say they're going to pull away from the shore and spend the afternoon fishing.'

'When are *we* having lunch?'

'Soon, but I must do a little exploring first.'
'All right, but don't be long.'

It is a wonderful thing, unencumbered by clothing, to come upon Greek and Roman remains under a hot sun. As I leave the dusty road I wander through imagined kitchens among the myrtle, and look for wild grapes in echoes of gardens. The dust and the pulse of warmth, the broken notes of unknown birds in old fig trees, the fragments of a fountain or cistern, all instill a timelessness that has seeped into the blood through Homer, Virgil and Ovid. 'The sleepy summer heat, the sea and the superb mountains, the contrast of the utter solitude with the busy life of the ancient city, combined to leave a memory not easily effaced.'* It may be true that historians give us circumstance and event, but it is only poetry that gets into the subconscious and recreates an apprehension of being.

'Well, what have you seen so far?' Duncan murmurs when I rouse him for lunch.

'Everything, and yet only the beginning. First there was the aqueduct. You can see part of it through those pine trees. It once marched over forest and gully and thrust out on the neck of that hill, which divided the town between three bays. Do you realise that Phaselis was a Greek city hundreds of years before the Romans took it over? It was founded from Rhodes in 690 BC, but even before that it was probably a trading post of the Phoenicians. Then for a time it was Persian, till 469 BC when, rather against its will though inhabited by Greeks, it was "liberated" by the Athenian general Cimon. When Alexander came on the scene – which was 333 BC – Phaselis was under Persian rule again, but he seems to have had no difficulty in persuading the Phaselitans to join him. Even before he arrived they sent him envoys with a golden crown.'

'What about the lake you were reading to me about?'

'Yes, that was fascinating. I walked across it. It's a dried-up swamp of dying marsh-grasses; the very same, I'm sure, that Livy spoke of, and Cicero too. Its baneful emanations were probably the cause of a disease that broke out among the Rhodian sailors when their fleet put in here in the first century BC. Livy noted the oppressive heat and the strange smells. Perhaps the sailors went swimming over the very ground I've just trod. Perhaps they drank the lake water as they swam. I did exactly that once in the Thames at Marlow on a broiling day.'

'Did anything happen to *you*?'

'Yes, I came down with paratyphoid.'

'Don, you're a foolish thing.'

'I know. I'm not exactly a safety-first person.'

'Go on with your travels.'

---

* George Bean, *Turkey's Southern Shore.*

'Leaving the marsh, I walked over the hot pebbles to the quay. I can't tell you how hot and dazzling the pebbles were. The quay leads to the ancient mole. It's a huge rampart of stonework that runs under the sea across the middle harbour. That's where we are now. Once the whole quay must have bristled with customs houses, warehouses and offices. It was a busy port. There are great blocks of stone everywhere. Can you imagine Phaselis at some high point of her history, swarming with sailors, diplomats and businessmen? It was a crucial city in the trade routes between East and West. All three harbours must have bustled with loading and unloading. Timber and dates, apparently, were two important commodities. And Phaselis was famous for attar-of-roses. Perhaps the scent of roses undid some of the mephitic smells from the lake. I expect there were lots of little restaurants and cooking-houses too, and a lovely smell of freshly frying fish.'

Duncan stirs from his comfortable lying position. 'I have an inkling it is time for lunch,' he says.

I unpack our feta and tomatoes and bread. 'What paradise!' I murmur, pouring us some wine.

'Yes,' he says, 'but I can't help feeling a little sad that I can only enjoy your explorations vicariously. Once I would have bounded over this ground as keen as you.'

'I know you would have.'

'Now I haven't the strength, and the ground is too uneven.'

'Never mind! My enthusiasm will do for two . . . By the way, one of our books says that when Pompey landed here a second time in 48 BC after his defeat by Caesar at Pharsalus in Thessaly, the citizens were outnumbered by the crew of Pompey's ships. The place had shrunk to nothing because of the pirates. 'Little Phaselis' the poet Lucan calls it in his *Pharsalia*. They'd made it their base. Rather sobering for poor Pompey, who in his brilliant days had obliterated the pirates from the whole of the Mediterranean in six weeks. Do you think he thought of the vanity of all human triumphs?'

'Undoubtedly.'

'Perhaps he knew he was on his way to being stabbed as he landed in Egypt.'

'I dare say he had something of a presentiment . . . as *I* had dreams a few weeks ago which made it quite clear to me I would not be given much longer.'

'Oh, Duncan, we all have dreams like that. Put away the thought. I want you to reach a hundred.'

'So that you can exhibit me?'

'Of course! I want to exhibit you as the Giant Panda.'

'You would!'

I see that the journey from Side in the heat has exhausted him more than I realised. After smoking a cigarette he lies down again on his soporific cushion of pine needles. The sun is lightly splashed around him, cooled by the trees, and he is in a pool of shade.

The life of the sea is fifteen yards away, with hardly a murmur. I have a whole after-noon of exploration before me.

'Have you come back, or are you not yet gone?' Duncan murmurs when I pass him on my way to the third bay an hour or so afterwards.

'Both . . . but go back to sleep. I'm not yet finished.'

'Before you leave me here for ever, tell me what you've been seeing.'

'I found a ruined cistern in the woods and couldn't help thinking it could easily be in the garden of Theodectes. He was a philosopher and lived in Phaselis in the fourth century BC. He was also a pupil of the more famous Isocrates. Did you know that Theodectes propounded his philosophy in riddles?'

'No. Tell me some.'

'What is large when it begins, small in middle life, large again towards its end?'

'I can't guess.'

'A shadow.'

'Here's another. There are two sisters. The first gives birth to the second, and the second to the first.'

'You know I'm no good at these things.'

'Night and day.'

'I found this bit of information in George Bean: "A statue of Theodectes stood in Phaselis, and one evening Alexander, roaming the streets with his companions after a good dinner, noticed the statue and in a mood of exhilaration, he was not an abstemious man, took the wreaths off his companions' heads and threw them on the statue; thereby paying, as Plutarch observes, a graceful compliment both to the philosopher and to his own association with philosophy through his tutor Aristotle." '

'A touching story.'

'Then I came to the road which I think connects Kemer, Phaselis and Olympus. I swung down that road thinking of Alexander's young Macedonians. They must have marched on the very same road on the eve of their big adventure; though Alexander himself with others of his troops seems to have waded along the shore towards Antalya.'

'Did *you* have any adventures?'

'Only this, that when a lorry came labouring up the hill I had to plunge like a wild goat into the undergrowth . . . You see, I didn't have a stitch on.'

'That's what I've come to expect.'

'Then I found a mysterious deep well on the wooded bluff which hangs over Phaselis. I could see no water in it, but through its tiny opening to the sky could tell how deep and spacious it was inside. Anyone who stumbled into it through the brambles would never be heard of again.'

'And I suppose you think that's consoling news to *me*!'

'Not exactly, but if I'd disappeared you'd simply have had to spend the rest of your days in Phaselis.'

'In a shepherd's hut no doubt.'

'As a matter of fact, I came upon the perfect spot: two huts made of wattle and brushwood. There were two empty bottles lying about, some chicken feathers and the ashes of a fire: all this only a stone's throw away from a series of huge block-like guard-rooms and a massive stone gate. The gate reminded me of the Lion Gate at Mycenae. A ramp broad enough for two chariots leads down towards the sea . . . It's funny but neither George Bean nor Kinross mentions it in either of their books.'

'Perhaps it's too hidden and they didn't explore as much as you have . . . what did you do then?'

'I slid on pine needles down the hill to the necropolis. You'd have found the spot very curious. On the brown banks of what looks like a dried-up torrent there's a whole valley of gutted tombs. It runs towards and sometimes parallel with the sea. The sarcophagi are of hewn stone, about six feet long and two and a half wide. They're all gutted and tossed here and there as if ransacked in a frenzy. Naturally I probed with a stick through a hole in one of them to see if there might be a jewel or a ring or a brooch which the robbers had overlooked.'

'That would have been a feather in your cap.'

'No such luck!'

I leave Duncan still reposing on his pine needles and stride across the neck of the isthmus which links the middle with the southern harbour. The Romans built a broad paved avenue running three hundred yards and flanked on either side by the remnants of houses, markets and temples which lie now deep in the growth of scrub and trees. So massive are the flagstones of this short road that even now hardly a tree has been able to push up between them.

Branching off to my right, I clamber over ruins and thickets to emerge from a brush of oleander on to the shores of the third bay. The afternoon is softening as I wade into the sea, walking over an ancient pier. I swim over smooth monolithic stones . . . But there are shouts. People are calling from the centre of Phaselis. It is our mariners looking for me.

'So here you are at last,' Duncan remarks with a look of relief as I run back to him through the scattered blocks of Hadrian's great gate 'Our sailors want us to embark.'

As our boat sputters and chortles over a sunset sea, I muse over all that is still left to explore: the theatre, the rectangular agora, perhaps even the shrine of Athena Polias, the chief deity of Phaselis, which has never been discovered. Perhaps then will be seen for the first time the spear of Achilles, its bronze point and butt once preserved there. And when I do return many years from now, I shall feel Duncan's presence in that pool of shade under the pine trees by the shore.

October 5th

We have set out to see more of the countryside. It is Duncan's first full review of the widely sprinkled village. I drive slowly and he takes everything in: the overhanging storeys of many of the squarish houses, the shaded gardens heavy with the green of walnut, pomegranate and mulberry, the small boys playing and the women washing clothes in the clear brisk runnels along the side of the road. The road deserts the shadows and coolness of the village and mounts into the hills, but after a mile or so it meets another road and this branches left towards the sea.

'This must be the road,' I say to Duncan, 'which leads to the mysterious Italian Shangri-La.'

'It may go nowhere at all,' he replies.

'It must. I'm sure it goes to the New Jerusalem I told you about.'

The road winds in and among the pines with respect and love. When it encounters a particularly fine tree, it divides, circles its arms around it and leaves the tree joyously intact.

'Only Italians could have built this road,' Duncan remarks. 'How I wish more roads behaved like this!'

'Amen to that . . . They say the Turks never cut down a tree.'

'So different from the Spanish!'

We talk about the francophile essence of Bloomsbury and I try to find words to say just why my pristine experience of his and Vanessa's pictures, the walled garden at Charleston, the fig trees in the patio, the hand-painted jugs and pots which figure in every still life, his and Vanessa's predilections in food and cooking, all crystalised for me in most telling symbols my own filial dedication to the Mediterranean.

'I just have to look at the olive trees in one of your sketches of Cassis or St Tropez, and a whiff of freshly baked croissants, just-caught sardines on the quay, a gulp of *vin ordinaire*, a plate of ham and figs, guzzling grapes six at a time, and all the classics, rush into my mind and my senses.'

'I'm sorry to hear of your gluttony with grapes,' Duncan comments, 'but the first time I set eyes on you – and even more, that first morning you lay prone on Edward le Bas' carpet for a painting – I saw that you came out of the Mediterranean.'

'No wonder neither of us specially cares for the Germans,' I laugh.

'I should think not – except for their music . . . but then, *you* don't care for music . . . a great pity!'

'What nonsense! I can only work with music in the background. And for me Beethoven is the King. I put him on the same pedestal as Sophocles and Shakespeare.'

'That's what I'd expect. For me nothing can compare with the humanity of Mozart.'

We have come to what looks like a frontier outpost: a sentry's cabin, a gate with an

101

elevating bar, three or four orderlies standing about: all proclaim the borders of a forbidden state. Duncan watches me get out of the car and put on an act of international charm in an attempt to break down their refusal to let us in: no simple overture because none of the guards speaks English, French or Italian. Smiles fail and now I pretend to be a student of modern architecture. No go either, but at least charm has leavened their grimness and they no longer look as if they might possibly shoot us. They even seem to be apologising for having their orders and I understand one of them to say: 'If only you had a permit from the Director, we'd be happy to open the gates to you.'

Now we are driving along our original course: a stony, pitted route that winds up and down hills and crosses dry river-beds. It must be the road to Phaselis, but I dare not press on there and risk our tyres on this cruel surface. We turn seawards down a track which runs parallel with a wide bay, pine needles and sand soothing our progress.

'I see no better place than this,' Duncan says. 'I think we should stop.'

'Yes, it's perfect for our alfresco.'

He settles himself with his sketchbook near the bole of an ancient pine, while I busy myself collecting that inevitable jetsam of plastic remnants, discarded cartons, old newspapers, soiled tissues which even on the shores of Southern Turkey desecrate every idyllic spot a car can reach.

'It won't take long,' I shout. 'There's not going to be an eyesore within a radius of a hundred yards.'

I add pine cones and dry sticks to my midden, and now the whole heap is blazing gloriously in the sun. Duncan continues to sketch so I climb up among the russet-coloured rocks that overlook the scene. On one side is the sea, dimpling along the shores of small deserted bays; on the other, or rather behind me, rise up the peaks of Mount Climax, Mount Olympus and Mount Phoenicus, that range of which Lord Kinross so well says: "... it is a flight of Gothic peaks, stylized in form, poetic in line, mounting in tiers to the sculptural climax which the Turks call Cabali Dag. Distilled into this luminous formal panorama is the essential Mediterranean, romantic and classical in one." '

Duncan has completed his charcoal sketch of the big pine tree. It is free and bold and brings out the tree's lonely stance. We sit by its massive girth, he leaning back against its bark, and I unfold our lunch of bread, feta cheese and tomatoes. The wine is a white Turkish of unknown provenance.

Duncan is silent. So am I. What is in my mind are those words of Roger Fry: 'Cézanne is so discreet, so little inclined to risk a definite statement for fear of being arrogant; he is so immensely humble; he never dares trust to his acquired knowledge; the conviction behind each brush stroke has to be won from nature at every step.' I cannot think of a better description of Duncan himself. I have watched him grapple with painting after painting, and always with the same air of challenge, hesitation and contemplation. He always approaches both his canvas and his subject with infinite precautions, 'stalking, as it were, now from one point of view, now from another', as Roger Fry says of Cézanne, 'and always in fear lest a premature definition might deprive it of something of its complexity.'

'Duncan, do you think drawing is important?'

He looks at me with something like consternation: 'Immensely, as you well know.'

'But you draw with such passion and despatch: not the way you paint at all.'

'I can't help that. One must capture completeness. A good drawing is "finished" after the first line. In painting there are so many more things to balance. It's contemplative.'

'You throw your drawings on the floor as if only the *act* of drawing was important.'

'Perhaps that's true.'

'And yet Cézanne couldn't really draw.'

Duncan looks at me, blinks and gives one of his incredulous chuckles, as if I had suggested the world was flat.

'Come on, you know very well he couldn't draw!'

'The answer isn't as easy as you think,' he begins. 'Cézanne had no facility in the ordinary business of getting verisimilitude, if that's what you mean. It was his organisation of planes and colour which made his achievement so magnificent.'

'Be that as it may, *your* achievement has been to paint with the solidity of Chardin and the structural design of Cézanne. I don't mean in your early decorative work – which short-sighted dealers and critics elect to prefer to your later work – but the canvases you began to master from the middle-1930s onwards. They have such simplicity and control, and you arrive at profounder truths without a hint of virtuosity.'

'Nice of you to say so! Especially when I sometimes think I can't paint at all and had better give up.'

'When Cézanne once said he'd like to start all over again but from nature – or something of that sort – d'you know what I think he meant?'

'I'm all agog.'

'He meant that he'd like to paint like you.'

Another of Duncan's incredulous chuckles.

'No, seriously. He knew he had never achieved that *ars est celare artem* which hides the method. His struggles to attain the truth of nature could never hide the way he was trying to do it. In *your* best work you do.'

'What nonsense you talk!'

'Say what you like, I know I'm right. In some of your later still-lifes one needs a magnifying glass to see how your brush-strokes build up chord after chord of harmony and truth. And yet your method is pure Cézanne.'

'Well, I hope there's something in what you say . . . Give me another glass of wine.'

While Duncan dozes against the pine, I have taken a series of photographs of us in this solitary spot, including one of a small adder that came sizzling over the gravel. It is the only snake I have seen in Turkey. But it is time to leave. A short storm broke over us while we sat under the pine tree. For three weeks we have had uninterrupted sun, and now the weather is on the change. Today is our last full day in Lycia and Pamphylia. Tomorrow we begin the first stage of our journey home.

October 6th

Last night during dinner under the pergola we were able to solve the garbled riddle of the Italians who had come, built a miniature city and left. Bacchus pointed out to me a man in his early thirties with marmalade sideburns who sat with four others at a neighbouring table.

'He's employed at the Italian colony and could answer all your questions.'

With encouragement from Duncan, I went over to their table, apologised for intruding and said: 'I'm curious to know about the Italian colony. What did they do?'

'What d'you mean "what did they do?"? What does anyone do?' answered Marmalade in an American accent.

'But what did they do before they left? I was told that the Italians have departed.'

'Of course they've departed. It's the end of the season.'

'But during the season who were they? What was it?'

'An *Italian holiday village.*'

He spelt the words out rudely as though I were a child.

'Oh, I thought it might have been some mining or engineering company.'

Marmalade, who I think was German, delved into his spaghetti.

I glanced across the tables towards Duncan. He would be disappointed with such jejune information; so I began again.

'I've been so struck with the whole design of the place that I long to visit it.'

'Then why don't you ask the Director? He's sitting over there.'

I turned to a man of young middle age with a round bushy beard. There was no malice in him and he answered me with a smile. 'Of course you and your father may visit the colony. It is my pleasure. Would half past ten tomorrow suit you? . . . I shall leave orders for the gate to be opened.'

Here we are, then, on the morning of our departure from Kemer, sitting on our beds with bowls of *caffè-latte* and the sun streaming in. We mean to visit Shangri-La before we leave. Duncan looks preoccupied and I know that the business of packing appals him. I distract him with an account of my afternoon walk along the sea yesterday when we had got back from our picnic.

'I came to a hedge of prickly pears in full fruit and I ate one: the first I've had since

Portrait of Paul Roche, 1958, collection of the author

The Turkish Café (from a sketch executed in Turkey), 1974, collection of Pandora Smith

my days in Mexico. Then I picked that sprig of black olives you see there in the glass.'

'I've been looking at it. It's magnificent.'

'Then I crossed a dry river-bed and did my exercises in the setting sun. I saw an old woman there kneeling behind a bush. She swayed and bowed towards the East, adoring Allah. Her goats ambled and nibbled all around her.'

'A lovely picture!' he says . . . 'I wish we didn't have to go.'

'There's one thing I want you to do, Duncan: sketch my olive sprig with its three black olives.'

'How can I? There simply isn't time.'

'There's masses of time: more than an hour. Besides, I'll do all the packing . . . Oh please! It'll be the symbol of our memories of Asia Minor.'

'Very well. I suppose I have to do what I'm told.'

'Yes, but with good grace. Your heart must be in it.'

The olive sprig is in a tumbler of water: the neat leaves still virginally turquoise and the three blue-black fruit glistening. I put it in various positions against the white of the wall. The sun, the dazzling white, and the sharp charcoal shadows etch a chiaroscuro fresco of their own.

'Doesn't it look lovely!' I remark.

'Certainly, but not for a drawing. The sun complicates things. And there's all the business of reflections in the glass.'

'I thought artists liked problems.'

'Not when they're given only ten minutes to solve them.'

Reluctantly, I prop the tumbler on a pillow in the shadows.

At 10.15, car loaded, bills paid, goodbyes said, olive sprig immemorially drawn, we drive off to see the Italian holiday town. There is no difficulty this time: guards salute, the gate swings up and we pass straight into Shangri-La. There are gardens everywhere, lawns, dew-ponds, masquerades of cannas, marigolds and zinnias. It all blends into the rocks and aromatic scrub of the hillside. Among it are piazzettas of polished travertine, rosettes of circular stairs leading to balconies, sudden terraces, turrets with shining windows angled towards the sea. Duncan is enchanted and sits gazing from the car.

'Aren't you going to get out?' I ask him.

'I think not. I can enjoy it all from here.'

I begin my own roaming through the white halls and up and down the towers. The place is like a film-set of a city in the outer galaxies, and empty. I push open doors and wander through a warren of sparkling bedrooms. Comfort and beauty are in the designs, and from every window one catches a facet of sea, mountain and garden.

'Did you see anyone at all?' Duncan asks when I reach him again.

'Yes, one single person. In a wide ambulacrum of empty offices I came upon a young man sitting at a desk.'

'Was he friendly?'

'Very. He told me the place was built by an Italian company called "Hotel-Clubs Valtur". It was only opened in June and the first batch of holiday-makers have just left. Most of them are Romans and Milanese, but anybody can come. I asked him if there was any way to guard against some ghastly Hilton rising up beside them. "None whatever," he said. "We only lease this site from the Turkish government. There's already a German scheme to build a similar holiday town on the bay east of us." "At least you've set them a high standard," I said.'

'Was he pleased with your compliment?'

'He seemed to be . . . Would you like to see something of the grounds?'

'Of course, but you know that's not possible.'

'Ah, but Nanny has found a way and Nanny is going to reward Master Duncan for waiting so patiently.'

'I hope Nanny knows what she's doing.'

I have in fact spotted a road that winds up and around the settlement. We drive through the gardens and come to a look-out over the ravines and towards the sea. I park the car on a slope. Behind us is a drop of twenty feet.

'I agree with you,' says Duncan, gazing over the sparkling panorama, 'great imagination has gone into the whole design.'

I start up the engine and release the handbrake. The car stalls and we slip towards the ravine. In a flash of terror I see every detail of a crumpled piece of tin-work that was once a car, and there among the rocks two glass-and-blood-spattered passengers lying backwards in their seats. Just as the wheels are on the point of spinning over space, I re-switch the starter, the car gives a jet-engine roar and we shoot up the hill.

'That was a noisy start!' says Duncan, oblivious of what we have just escaped.

So we are on our way to Antalya, already bumping like a stagecoach on the cruellest of roads that seems to go on for ever. All my old dreads of breaking down assail me but I distract Duncan with endless prattle about the fields, the crops, the nature of the cotton plant. The day is hot but the sea is not composed. Yesterday's storm has annoyed it and it still shows its fangs.

'Duncan, when you were sent home to England from India, how old were you?'

'About nine.'

'So was I.'

'My grannie was at Southampton to meet me: my father's mother, you know, the one who ran off with a lover twice in the Himalayas and produced Uncle George and Aunt Hennie.'

'Oh that grannie, the interesting grannie!'

'Yes, she had a lovely old house in Chiswick, Hogarth House. I lived with her and found her delightful. Everything she said interested me. When she died a few years later, I used to go and stay with Uncle George who lived at Winchester. I never took to him. He was a retired Indian civil servant and the only one of my father's brothers who wasn't musical. He had a son called "White Pat" to distinguish him from Uncle Charles's son "Black Pat". Black Pat was very naughty and had several affairs, including one with Ailie, White Pat's wife.'

'Tell me again who Uncle Trevor was.'

'He was the brother who was eaten by a bear. He had four or five sons who stayed mostly in India. Uncle Trevor was married to a half-caste lady, and a huge enlarged photograph of her stood on an easel in his sitting-room. He read practically all night and Mrs Masters his housekeeper gave him a sort of breakfast-lunch at about twelve or one. When he was not reading he used to play the cello for hours together. I thought him very flirtatious with his Strachey nieces, and I remember him with his hand nearly always around Pippa's waist.'

'What about Charles?'

'He was retired from the army and published songs. He married a clever Jewess, Aunt Aggy. My mother couldn't bear her and thought she was a mischief-maker, which I think was true. "She is a Becky Sharp," I was told.'

We must be half-way to Antalya and are now driving between the sea and fields of cotton.

'Would you like to see some cotton?' I ask.

'Is there any?'

'It's all around us.'

'Oh, I thought they were white poppies.'

I get out of the car and pick a sprig of bursting cotton bolls.

'There, Duncan, that's cotton, actual cotton.'

We open a bottle of wine and I ask him if the scenery is like any place he knows.

'No, but if the maize fields were oats and there was heather growing under the pine trees and the mountains weren't so big, I might think of Rothiemurchus.'

'Your birthplace.'

'Where I spent several summers as a boy. And I remember my grandfather, the one who had been Governor of Jamaica, being wheeled about in a bath-chair. He lived in a different wing from my grandmother. They led completely separate lives.'

'What happened to you when the South African War broke out? Didn't your father have to join his old regiment in Malta?'

'He did and I went to stay with my Strachey cousins in London. Aunt Janie, Lady Richard Strachey, was my father's sister. It's a pity he had to go to Malta because he was enjoying conducting the orchestra of a travelling company of musical comedy.'

'He was good enough for that, was he?'

'He was a first-rate musician. Much too good for that, but he did it very well.'

'Would you say he wasn't really fitted for the army?'

'Not at all. He was too educated and too civilised. His interests were always in other things. In Burma, for instance, he wrote a book which has become a classic.'

'I know, you gave me a copy: *The Orchids of Burma* . . . Duncan, your father sounds an attractive man.'

'He was, and music was his passion. He and his brothers were friends of Joachim and his quartet, especially of Piatti the cellist, who once took me on his knee at the age of four and promised to make a good cellist of me.'

'I believe your father used to get up an orchestra in his regiment.'

'He did. Wherever he went there was music. He used to do things for the theatre too . . . a very gifted man but I never got to know him intimately. I think he thought me rather a nuisance. Indeed, I was. He loved pretty women and he loved music. He, Janie, his brothers and Aunt Lell [Elinor] could argue by the hour about music . . . He became manager of the Royal Artillery Mess at Woolwich.'

I asked Duncan if he thought it sadly ironic that such a beautiful pair as Bartle and Ethel, his parents, should so soon have fallen out of love.

'Yes, but I don't think they were ever sad about it,' he said. 'With my father affairs were inevitable and my mother accepted the fact. No one thought ill of her for going her own way too.'

'I seem to remember your telling me that even in Malta she was making a hit with the officers.'

'Indeed, the Commander-in-Chief, Admiral Fisher, insisted on dancing with her every evening.'

'In front of your father's eyes?'

'In front of everyone's eyes.'

'Wasn't she in love with Commander Young then?'

'That made no difference. It was a flirtation. An outrageous flirtation.'

'Not going as far as to bed?'

'I don't think so, because Lady Fisher used to laugh at it too. Everybody laughed at it, but it was quite a serious flirtation.'

We are leaving the plain now and climbing up on to the cliff where the road-making lorry swung into our rear four days ago. Soon the bay of Antalya will come into sight. Suddenly, rumbling towards us with only inches to spare, comes the very same lorry. I recognise its shape and dirty brown sides.

'Quick Duncan, a pencil. We've got its number: PA 6973.'

'But there is no pencil.'

'PA 6973, PA 6973,' I go on reciting like a mantra while I stop the car and find a pencil. Then on the back of a piece of carton Duncan writes PA 6973.

'For once in my life,' I tell him, 'I feel I've done the smart thing. It'll come in useful when we face the Genco Car Hire Service and hand in this battered Fiat.'

Our so lately simple life in Kemer already seems like a dream. It is now 5.30 in the evening. In the same car, we are actually heading for the airport. The last six hours in Antalya have passed pleasantly enough. After lunch in the Hotel Perge, Duncan settled himself in an armchair and I ran down the steep steps of the marina for a last sunbathe and a plunge.

Later, we inched our way through the thickening traffic to do some eleventh-hour shopping. Every street, alley and alcove was thick with pedestrians, bicycles, barrows, marketeers, children. It surprised me how quickly I became as callous as any Turk behind the wheel: hooting at old women, barging within a millimetre of a baby's pram, scattering chickens under our wheels. It was either this or being too scared to move. We left the car in a backwater and walked slowly through that extraordinary emporium of ancient handicrafts – leather-workers, smithies, jewellers – and modern trash: shiny threadbare shoddy, plaster kitsch, cheap furniture, and the inevitable plastic shoes. We stopped at my friend the harness-maker's, where Duncan bought some glass horse-beads for a present and we were constrained for politeness's sake to drink small cups of milkless tea.

Earlier in the afternoon I had confronted the Genco Car Hire Service. My friend and I think ally, Sirma Subutayi, was not in the office. She was taking a party of tourists round Europe, a young man said. I saw that it was hopeless to wrangle. Three Turkish mechanics were ranged against me. They all swore that the breakdown of the dirty red Fiat in Side was entirely my fault. In spite of the most complete insurance one can buy, I was forced to shell out 950 lira, which is about £30. However, I scored a minor triumph, a pyrrhic victory.

'What happens if the damage is done by somebody else?' I asked. 'Does the insurance pay up then?'

'But of course.'

'Then come and look at what someone did to your white Fiat.'

Like a batch of startled monkeys they whipped round to the back of the parked Fiat in which Duncan was still sitting.

'Look,' I said, pointing to the dent in the rear mudguard and the four smashed squiggly defunct lights. 'Done by a lorry in a mountain pass. His number is PA 6973.'

We cannot be far from the airport now, but ever since my final dip in the Mediterranean the thunder clouds have been massing and at last they break. In a few moments the road is a river. A virulent spray from the tarmac covers our headlights as we crawl through the dark. Duncan looks uneasy. 'Do you know where you're going?' he says. 'Of course!' At a garage my guess is confirmed. 'Keep going till you see a sign to the right,' they tell us.

We are at the airport now, sitting in the car and waiting for the floods to abate. It gives me the opportunity to open six small tins of tomato juice and to mix our bloody marys for the next two days. I make it half and half.

October 7th

Our last day in Turkey. The plane for London from Istanbul leaves at 4.15 this afternoon; which means we must depart for the airport at about 2.30. It is Sunday, and raining. The very word 'airport' has come to have an ominous ring. Yesterday evening our sojourn in the airport at Antalya lasted two hours. However, the large waiting-room there was comfortable. Duncan sat sipping coffee laced with cognac and I bloody marys. We were both very near a state of trance as we watched the extraordinary cross-section of humanity which was a whole waiting plane-load: there were prosperous businessmen strutting up and down discussing deals; cuddling honeymoon couples, peasant families spreading out their picnics before them, and children romping. But even without this passing show, one could never be bored in Duncan's company. At the age of nearly ninety the interest of his alert soul made itself present in everything. There was never a platitudinous remark, and always the unexpected comment. I found myself asking him about his association with Jacques Copeau at the Vieux Colombier theatre in Paris.

'We met in London,' he told me, 'and he invited me to design the clothes for *La Nuit des Rois, ou Que Voulez-Vous?*. So I went to Paris and was enraptured with the effervescence and enthusiasm of Copeau, and with the charm of the company. There was that great actor Jouvet, who looked like a naughty schoolboy; Tessier, a figurante; Albane almost *trop bonne*, and Dullin always right.'

'Was Copeau himself a great actor?'

'I think not. He was too intelligent: that is, one was too conscious of his intelligence. He almost made you realise what he *thought* of his role while he was playing it. In a play like Mérimée's *La Carosse du Saint Sacrement* he was inimitable. His appreciation of the adroitness and wit of his part was contagious. It was wit illuminated by wit . . . rather rare on the stage.'

'I wonder what you mean by a "great actor" then?'

'I'm thinking perhaps too much of those legendary figures of the past. To me the ghost of Irving is a very real thing, and though I never saw him I was told by my educated relations who had that Irving was a miserable, contorted, uneducated mountebank . . . And then there is the ghost of Kean and the ghost of Mrs Siddons and of Garrick. What one reads about their performances sometimes gives me the gravest doubts about what I would have thought of them . . . I'm thinking too of nearer magnificences. I myself have been overcome by performances. I saw Duse act *The Lady from the Sea* in the Tottenham Court Road – on her way to her death in cold America. It was wonderful, but when she was not on the stage all was desolate.'

'Did Copeau ever talk to you about the theatre?'

'Constantly, and about the great actors of the past. He had a real feeling for the magic of the actor, though his own performances went beyond a purely acting

110

interest. For one thing, he understood the literary qualities of a play and its whole bearing on the life of today or yesterday: a thing, I suppose, utterly foreign to the great actor-managers of the past and more like the ideas of Stanislavsky in Moscow; but I'm very ignorant here. New ideas were certainly in the air in 1914 . . . Barker in England was already making Shakespeare a living author and Shaw a revived one. At the same time, Copeau in his little hut held all the strings in his hand. Copeau's genius was to make the drama of any age come alive. His view of a whole play was magnificent, and with what patience did he not produce his idea! It was a glorious moment not only for plays long put aside as unbearably out of date, but a glorious moment for actors too.'

I asked Duncan about Michel Saint-Denis as a director, knowing how much he admired him.

'Yes indeed. I met him first selling tickets behind the guichet at the Vieux Colombier when I was working on the costumes for *Twelfth Night*. He was a relative of Copeau and working with him enthusiastically. After that I was aware of his constant presence behind the scenes. I lost sight of him till the Compagnie des Quinze came to London after the First War. I was delighted to see him and to see that he was carrying on the traditions of the Vieux Colombier. I also met Dasté, Copeau's daughter, who sat to me for her portrait – as did the great Tessier long before, after a performance.'

It was well after ten o'clock last night when we landed and made for Istanbul by taxi. In my pocket I had a list of three of the most suitable hotels: the Konak, the Perge, the Keban. The drive into town took about twenty-five minutes. The Konak was full up. We proceeded to the Perge. The Perge was full up; we searched out the Keban. The Keban turned us down. It was raining and we had had no dinner. We roamed onwards. At last in an obscure street we came upon a shabby place called the Sheba.

'Not exactly the Ritz,' I called to Duncan from the porch. 'It's moth-eaten and possibly flea-bitten but they can have us. In fact, they're already bowing and scraping.'

'Perhaps we're their only guests,' said Duncan.

Several people came forward to pick up our bags. We hurried through the drizzle, huddled for a short time in our decrepit chamber, and then went out in search of dinner. There was a restaurant a hundred yards from the Sheba. 'Rather scruffy,' I said to Duncan. 'Yes, but at least it's alive,' he replied.

Indeed, most of the diners were students: earnest young men talking economics, liberated girls with their beaux, and between them all plenty of catcalls and laughter.

'What's your soup like, Duncan?'

'Excellent. What's your boiled lamb like?'

'Execrable. The lamb must have been young in the days of Kemal Ataturk.'

I see Duncan gazing at the head of a dark young man three tables away: a saturnine head with a shock of black curls and eyes as impenetrable as obsidian. Yes, a fine head without being exactly beautiful. Duncan has put on his portrait-painting look, which means he stares unblinkingly in one direction with a gaze both wonderstruck and analytic, as if he were watching the unfolding of a sunset. The person he scrutinises turns into an object to be assessed, measured, balanced against all the subtleties of light and shade. His long, exquisite fingers seem to be holding something and there are tentative movements as though he were about to trace an outline on the table-cloth with brush or charcoal.

'I pity anyone you choose to do a portrait of,' I say tauntingly.

Duncan looks away from his subject and grunts.

'Yes,' I go on, 'the sittings become unending. Most of your portraits are marvellous after about the third sitting. By the thirty-third they're ruined.'

'That can't be helped,' he answers. 'It's better to ruin a picture than not to have pushed it as far as one wants.'

'Maybe, but it's a shame, and the wretched model feels he has been a sitting-victim all for nothing.'

'What nonsense you talk! Besides, one can never have enough sittings.'

The wine we are drinking, and even the tough old sheep which I have almost got through, has put new heart into me. Duncan too is recovering from the journey and is, I judge, robust enough to take a little teasing. A memory has struck me. I begin by reminding him of the long-drawn-out and nightmarish charade he enacted with a certain countess.

* * * * *

It all began some eight or nine years ago when our midweek sittings in Victoria Square (where Leonard Woolf rented him a top-storey flat) came to be interrupted by Duncan's saying, in a far from enthusiastic voice:

'I'm afraid you'll have to have lunch on your own today. I've got another session with the Earl.'

'Oh! How is your portrait going?'

'It isn't.'

'Never mind, at least you'll be given a good lunch.'

'Not a bit of it! I'll be lucky if I get sardines on toast.'

'What's wrong with the portrait?'

'The countess keeps a hawk's eye on every brush-stroke. She wants an exact replica of her husband.'

'Does she say things like: "The left eyebrow is too high" and "Don't you think the nose needs to be longer?"?'

'That's the sort of thing.'

'But I do think a portrait should look like the person it's supposed to be.'

'Perhaps, but that doesn't always make it a good painting.'

These sittings might have become a weekly event had they not been brought to a halt, *per forza*, by the decease of the Earl. Two years went by and then something else began to happen . . .

'Don, I'm afraid you'll have to have lunch on your own today.'

'Oh!'

'Yes. The Countess wants me to go to her place . . . Do you remember my doing that portrait of her husband? Well, she's hauled it out and wants me to alter the eyes and the lips.'

'At least you'll get a decent lunch.'

'Not a bit of it! I'll be lucky if it's sardines on toast. She lives all on her own now, somewhere near Millbank.'

After this had happened two or three times, I said to him: 'Why don't you bring the blessed thing here?' (Duncan had by then moved to a flat in Pat Trevor-Roper's basement at 3 Park Square West, off Regents Park.)

'Yes,' he said, 'I think I'd better. At least I won't have to confront the Countess every time.'

And so the picture was brought to Duncan's flat. That was when I first caught sight of his portrait of the Earl. Whether it looked like the distinguished diplomat or not I could not say, but it struck me as a good solid piece of work: the colours muted, almost sombre, but warm and alive. We propped the picture up on a chair in our one big studio room and Duncan got his brushes out. The tinkering began. After each onslaught I noticed he quickly turned the picture to the wall.

'It's going from bad to worse,' he murmured.

After lunch, while he was washing up, I sneaked a look. Undoubtedly the metamorphosis of the Earl was on its way. The torso remained untouched but the head had shrunk. I put it back against the wall and said nothing.

After some weeks of this – intermittent weeks because there were always his four or five days at Charleston – Duncan blurted out: 'I'm in despair.'

'You mean the Earl?'

'Yes. He hangs over me like a pall. Don't laugh. Life's hardly worth living.'

'And you're not being paid a penny, are you?'

'That's the least of my worries.'

Then one day Angelica came by and blithely said: 'Oh Duncan, don't worry. I'll take it on.'

True to her word, she went off with the canvas. I must say I thought her painterly confidence remarkable. Perhaps she really couched her willingness to come to the rescue in more diffident terms, but I remember only Duncan's sigh of relief. It seemed to him that all his troubles were over.

'It's so difficult to match one's colours after a painting is done and put away with,' he remarked.

A few weeks later, when I went to meet him at Victoria Station, I noticed an oblique, quizzical light in his eyes and a hesitation of manner greater than usual — like a sort of tension between hopelessness and euphoria.

'Angelica's given up on the Earl,' he muttered. 'She's passed him on to Fanny Garnett . . . Fanny is equal to anything.'

It was about a month later that Duncan staggered downstairs carrying the now familiar canvas under his arm. He looked beaten.

'Fanny has given up on it,' he said.

He had no need to add: 'And so have I.' Nor had he the heart to 'unveil' the picture. *I* did that.

What I beheld filled me with hilarious dismay. The torso remained untouched, but the process of shrinking the head had been pushed to an extreme. And the neck had grown. The expression on the Earl's features at the end of it hardly mattered because the whole cephalogical landscape had become reduced to a cellar-pale Chinesey face arching out of a body and shoulders much too big for it. I laughed.

'Did you ever see a film called *Creatures of the Lost World*?' I asked.

'I think I did. An ancient film.'

'Well, there was a mammoth beast in it with a long neck, tiny head, and enormous body. It ate only vegetables. That's what you've turned the Earl into.'

In spite of himself Duncan laughed too.

'I see what you mean,' he said, 'but I can do no more. I dare do no more.'

I tried to console him. 'If you look at it fixedly,' I said, 'it does begin to acquire its own kind of credibility.'

'The credibility of the Loch Ness Monster,' he replied.

Laughter aside, a day had to be set for returning 'Nessie' to the Countess. Duncan went ahead with the plans with admirable composure. Nevertheless, I thought I had better be there. We went by taxi to the flat in Millbank — the picture propped up between my knees. The Countess herself opened the door. It was a flat on the ground floor. She ushered us in as I took good care to keep the picture from view. I judged her to be about sixty-five: greyish hair, aquiline features, pleasant, simple in manner. On Duncan's features hovered an expression between forced nonchalance and nervousness. It was as if he hoped that at the last minute, *per impossibilità*, some alchemy would change the Loch Ness Monster into a ravishing memory of the lady's husband. What gave the tension irony — an irony she could not have guessed at but which tautened our apprehension unbearably — was that every moment of polite dalliance led her to suppose that the problem of her husband's portrait had been beautifully solved, whereas we knew it was now beyond solution: human, angelic or divine. We ought to have revealed the picture to her at the front door; instead, there we were urbanely stalling while being offered sherry and shown numerous portraits and photographs of the Earl. When the Countess was busy getting the sherry glasses, I whispered to Duncan: 'I see exactly what she wants: a coloured photograph.'

'It's too late, too late!' he answered miserably.

'Shall we go into the dining-room?' suggested the Countess. 'The light is better there.'

She pointed to a space on the wall.

'That's where I'm thinking of hanging it. Would it look well there?'

Poor Duncan, hardly capable of saying 'Yes', came out with something between a groan and a bleat. Even that did not put the lady on her guard. Slowly I took the picture from where I had placed it with its face to the wall. The moment had come.

* * * * *

'Duncan, do you remember what happened then?' (He was trying to peel a pear, stone hard.)

'Do I not! The moment is indelible.'

I took the pear from him . . . Yes, the moment was indelible. In one brisk movement I had swung the portrait into view. The Countess reeled and, before she could stop herself, the words were out.

'Ohhh! . . . It's horrible! Quite horrible!'

I handed Duncan's pear back to him, peeled and quartered. He was laughing, but as much with embarrassment as with merriment.

'The poor woman!'

'Yes, "the poor woman" you may well say. Appalled at what she had just uttered to the Master himself, she tried to cover it with: "Oh, no no no! I didn't mean that. I'm sure in its own way it's a masterpiece", but each time her eyes fell upon Loch Ness Monster, the words burst out: "Horrible! Quite horrible!" She was caught in a vice of compulsions: to tell the truth and to remain polite.'

'Do you remember how we ever got out?' Duncan asked.

'Not really. I know we were pretty nippy. I beat it to the front door on the pretext of finding a taxi, and I think I heard you mumbling something about one day having another go.'

I looked at Duncan with mock seriousness.

'There's still time, you know.'

'Oh no, not that! Never again. Never, never!' . . .

'Shall we have some coffee?'

'Of course.'

As we ordered it I saw the saturnine young man, who had indirectly prompted these memories, rise from the table and lead his girl out. Duncan's eyes followed them.

We were not back in our room till about 12.30. As Duncan undressed I noticed he had grazed his shin. I did not like the look of it and I applied some ointment and a plaster. I too had a wound. The foot which the rocks at Side had taken a sliver off was, in spite of all the sun and salt water, beginning to fester.

Duncan lay down in his bed and I tucked him up. The last thing I heard him say was: 'We mustn't get up late. There's so much to see and we only have half a day.'

I went to sleep marvelling at his energy. And his eagerness was like a child's. It was sixty-five years since his first visit to Istanbul with Maynard Keynes.

It is about 8.30 a.m. We are drinking *caffè-latte* in the Hotel Keban, which is thick with the guttural hubbub of lower-middle-class Germans.

'Thank God we didn't stay here!' Duncan remarks.

'I know. Let's flee.'

We have done just that and are now getting out of a cab outside Santa Sophia. The rain of last night is petering out and we step gingerly between streams and puddles on our way to the southern door of the basilica. There are crowds everywhere. The gravely beautiful Madonna in the mosaiced arch which spans the entrance, with the Emperors Justinian and Constantine on either side of her, gazes down at us as though moving forward to meet the world. 'You do not look at the Virgin,' someone has said, '*she* looks at *you*.'

We walk into the huge edifice tremulously. Duncan is overwhelmed by memories: a young man's in his early twenties. He sees again — and I for the first time — that miraculous lift of domes and half-domes which floats so luminously. The space makes me compare it with St Peter's, but in St Peter's the space seems somehow captured and anchored. Here space floats in space. The wide domes could be flying saucers, incandescent with light from a litany of windows. The place soars.

Groups of tourists, harangued by their guides, stand and strain and goggle. Duncan and I sidle up to one such group hoping for free scholarly pickings. It is Russian and we edge away. He sits down for some minutes on the steps of a mighty font, then we attach ourselves to a group of Italians, from whose guide we learn that a cold current of air from a certain doorway is one of the minor wonders of Santa Sophia. 'This cooling draught never ceases,' he says, 'even when the temperature outside is over ninety.'

Now we have set ourselves to walk up a long sloping ramp behind the sanctuary. It turns and turns endlessly up towards the gallery.

'Duncan, do you really want to do this? There's nowhere to sit down.'

'I do.'

The climb takes a quarter of an hour and we are both limping. Once in the gallery, Duncan rests and I wander. An English video company is televising the mosaics. The arc-lamps turn a lugubrious St John the Baptist clad in green into a scintillating Proteus rising from the sea. Through the high windows, if one stands on tiptoe, one can catch glimpses of facets of Byzantium: a swathe of blue bay, the sun catching the leaves of a fig tree as it gropes upwards out of a patio of shadows, a garden lined with Greek statues.

We emerge from Santa Sophia into the light. The clouds have gone. I take a photograph of Duncan sitting on a marble step and then go to look at a cluster of seventeenth-century villas and kiosks in the mosque's precincts. They are fretted with high windows, and the overhanging loggias look down on little gardens in the shade of ancient mulberries. I see the tomb of Suleiman the Magnificent, a contemporary of Queen Elizabeth who, with his great architect Mirmur Sinan, transformed the Greek city of Byzantium into the Ottoman capital, Istanbul: filling it with mosques, palaces, bridges, aqueducts, schools and hospitals.

On my return to Duncan, he announces: 'Now we must visit the Blue Mosque', the Blue Mosque being the popular name for the Mosque of Sultan Ahmet built in 1616. We can see its dome about five hundred yards away rising up among a congeries of lesser domes and minarets.

'We can walk there,' he says. 'It's so close.'

'But think of all the walking we'll have to do when we get there! And we're both hobbling.'

Against his inclinations we take a taxi, and it is well we have done so. The main entrance is no longer by the great door and we have been constrained to make an enormous detour round the central court, walking very slowly.

Once inside, in our stocking feet, we find ourselves treading on a prairie of carpets. All is softness, silence and colour. A blaze of blue tiles and stained glass hits the eye as flamboyant as a peacock's tail, and yet, in spite of the grandeur, the place is warm and comforting.

'Remarkable, but not to be compared with Santa Sophia,' Duncan murmurs.

'Certainly not, but impressive in its way.'

'A pity the pillars are so thick!' he comments. 'Rather vulgar.'

'I agree. I suppose they have to take a great weight.'

We wander through gallery and alcove. Although other sightseers are doing the same, the air is hushed, people pray. We come upon a group of six Muslim nuns veiled in white muslin, some squatting, some seated. They read and pray.

'Just look at *him*,' I call to Duncan.

It is an old man kneeling on a mint-green carpet. His head is swathed in a white turban. An amber-coloured mantle falls to the ground. He holds in his hands an ancient Koran, open.

Duncan's eyes light up. 'How Delacroix would have loved him!' he whispers.

We hail a cab outside the Blue Mosque and there ensues a charade in which I try to get the driver to understand – in English, French and Italian – that we want to be taken to a thoroughly Turkish restaurant: 'You know, where no tourists go.' Just as we are about to give up hope, a slight, dark young man, pleasant but not good-looking, comes forward and politely asks in English if he can help. Obviously delighted to practise his English he sits down in the taxi between Duncan and me and off we go. He tells us he is studying for his baccalaureate.

'My father is not rich. I live with my uncle: a hard man and a miser. He makes jewellery out of gold and I help him.'

'What will you do after your degree?' I ask.

'I'd like to become a doctor. But I don't want to stay in Turkey.'

'Are the walls of Byzantium still standing?' Duncan asks.

'In places, yes, but new buildings encroach them.'

Duncan tells him how once long ago he rode round the walls on horseback with Maynard Keynes.

'He's nearing ninety,' I whisper to the young man, whose eyes fill with reverence.

Our student, whose name is Aydin Tasci, has taken us to a restaurant. It is zealously Muslim and there is no wine. Duncan toys with a watery soup and I stare at my indifferent hors-d'oeuvre.

'Let's go somewhere else,' I whisper.

'Yes, but we'd better pretend to eat what we've ordered.'

On my finger I sport the 'Byzantine' ring I exchanged in Side for my electric razor. I hold it out to Aydin.

'Cast in a mould, not carved,' he says dismissively, 'and not gold.'

Duncan's eyes twinkle naughtily as I hide my hand under the table.

We move off slowly to a second restaurant some hundred yards away. There there is wine, but now we have no appetite. We eat melon and Aydin consents to an ice-cream. It is nearing the time we should return to the Sheba and get our things together. Aydin insists on coming with us. When I tell him that we want to buy vodka, raki and cognac to take back to England, he says: 'I know where to find them.'

The time is about a quarter to three and we are speeding through the suburbs on our way to the airport. The last hour has passed full of apprehension for both of us: Duncan sitting in an armchair at the Sheba, thinking I was lost or kidnapped, and I combing Istanbul with Aydin for a liquor shop that was open. It being a Sunday, all the places that he knew were shut. We walked and walked: past pyramids of eggs in the market, and cornucopias of fruit and vegetables, dodging into shop after shop. Just as I was about to say: 'Look, it doesn't matter. We must be at the airport in half an hour', Aydin plunged into a small grocery and out again announcing: 'Yes, they have vodka, cognac, raki.'

Duncan looks tired. He turns to me and says: 'For a moment I thought he'd insist on coming with us . . . I don't think I could have kept another conversation going.'

'I didn't know what to give him. I only had a 500-lira note in my pocket. I've promised to send him some English stamps,' I say.

The open plain we are driving through should be a countryside of fields, crops and pastures but it has already caught the disease of urban sprawl. It is like the outskirts of an American town: the same rash of petrol stations and dumped car cemeteries, the same conglomeration of sitings without architectural cohesion, the same assault of vulgarity in billboards.

'It's not what one would expect of Byzantium,' Duncan remarks.

'I should think not. We're coming to the logical conclusion of an evil system. Ezra Pound's being proved right.'

'What did *he* say?'

'That our whole economy is based on usury. Money has become more important than what it's supposed to represent. We can't feed the starving thousands with our gargantuan surpluses of wheat because that would affect the price of wheat in Wall Street. To keep prices high we must maintain, if not create, shortages. Meanwhile, ugliness and pollution spawn like a virus.'

'You sound angry.'

'I am.'

'Well, don't be so angry that you can't enjoy all that's still good and beautiful. Think of Santa Sophia.'

On our passage through the airport, which is surprisingly brisk, I am dealt a final blow to my faith in the honesty of the *patron* of the Pamphylia. There, laid out in rows, are a score of Byzantine pendant crosses identical with my own; their price a tenth of what I paid. I keep this quiet from Duncan as he looks on suspiciously while I get rid of my last lira buying a jewelled dagger for my son Pote.

'I should have thought you'd wasted enough money,' I hear him murmur. 'Perhaps you despise money by getting rid of it!'

We are in the air at last — oh the blessedness of sinking back! — both too exhausted for conversation. However, when the drinks come round, I cannot resist seeing if I can strike from Duncan his usual sparkle. 'Do you propose rousing yourself sufficiently from your torpor to toast the Turks?' I tease.

'A neat whiskey,' he retorts dreamily.

Later when the dinner trays are passed around and he refuses his, I try again.

'Master Duncan, this is naughty. Nanny is not pleased. Dinner is succulent little chops. You might at least have given me yours.'

'I'm well aware of Nanny's appetite,' he replies.

'But whiskey on an empty stomach is disastrous.'

'So you say!'

When I next turn to look at him, Duncan is asleep.

October 17th

We have been back in Aldermaston ten days now and we have both been ill. At first Duncan just lay in bed and slept, but these last few days he has been drawing with pastels, propped up on pillows. This morning he is sitting in an armchair sketching my anthurium on the window sill. On the first night of our arrival he pulled himself out of bed several times during the night and wandered down the corridor in search of our bathroom in Side.

'Duncan, whatever are you doing?' I called from my mattress on the floor.

'Maynard's arriving by train from Cambridge and I promised to meet him.'

After his third day of being in bed, and mine of limping with a swollen foot, I thought it absurd not to call in Dr Cooper, our village doctor who lives across the street. I pretended to Duncan that it was only to look at our legs. 'I'm lame,' I said, 'and your shin isn't getting any better.'

Dr Cooper sized up the situation. Everything could be blamed on the grazed shin. 'It's infected,' he said, 'and that's what you're suffering from.' Having given Duncan a thorough check-up from top to toe, he prescribed him an ointment and a powerful course of pills.

When my turn came I peeled off my sock and the doctor took my foot in his hands with a look of concern. The part where the skin had been shaved off by the rock had developed into an inverted cone like a small volcano, running deep into the flesh.

'You are both suffering from the same infection,' the doctor said, 'and yours, Paul, is much the worse.'

It was a clever thing for him to say, for it made Duncan feel by far the robuster of the two. Which, of course, he *is*.

Dates in the Life of Duncan Grant

1885   21 January   Duncan James Corrowr Grant born at Rothiemurchus, Inverness-shire, only child of Major Bartle Grant, 8th Hussars, and Ethel Grant (née McNeil); a few months later the family move to Canterbury.

1887–94   Lives in India and Burma, returning to England every two years. Educated by a governess, Alice Bates.

1894–9   At Hillbrow Preparatory School, Rugby. Rupert Brooke a fellow pupil. Spends his holidays with his grandmother, Lady Grant, at Hogarth House, Chiswick.

1899 April –
1901 December   Attends St Paul's School, London (for two terms as a boarder). Wins several art prizes. Intended for an army career, but his parents are persuaded by his aunt, Lady Strachey, to allow him to study art.

1899/1900–6   Lives with Sir Richard and Lady Strachey and their children.

1902–5   Attends Westminster School of Art. Encouraged in his studies by Simon Bussy, a lifelong friend of Matisse, who married Dorothy Strachey, Grant's cousin.

1904–5 Winter   Visits Italy. Copies part of the Masaccio frescoes in Sta Maria del Carmine, Florence (as a commission for Harry Strachey), and the portrait of Federico da Montefeltro in the Uffizi. Greatly impressed by the frescoes of Piero della

Francesca in S. Francesco, Arezzo. Sometime between 1903 and 1905, on the advice of Simon Bussy, he makes a copy of the angel musicians in Piero della Francesca's *Nativity* in the National Gallery, London.

1905	Late	Introduced to Vanessa Stephen by Pippa Strachey at the Friday Club.
1906	February	After gift of £100 from an aunt, spends two years in Paris studying at La Palette, J.-E. Blanche's school. Visits the Luxembourg and sees the Caillebotte Bequest of French Impressionist and other paintings.
	June	Visits Florence and Siena.
1907		Continues studies in Paris until the summer.
	Easter	In Paris with Clive and Vanessa Bell and Virginia Stephen.
	Autumn	Spends part of the autumn term at the Slade School of Art (also recorded there in the summer term of 1908). On return to England becomes a friend of J.M. Keynes (later Lord Keynes), the economist.
1908		Spends two months in the Orkneys on holiday with J.M. Keynes and paints his portrait; also visits Rothiemurchus.
c. 1908–9		Visits Leo and Gertrude Stein for the first time. Sees their collection of paintings by Picasso and Matisse.
1909	Summer	With an introduction from Simon Bussy, visits Matisse.
	October	Shares rooms with Keynes at Belgrave Road, London. Later moves to 21 Fitzroy Square. Exhibits two works at the New English Art Club exhibition.
c. 1909–14		Several visits to Picasso's studio. (Grant visited Paris frequently before the outbreak of war in 1914.)

1910	10 February	Takes part in the *Dreadnought* hoax with Horace Cole, Adrian and Virginia Stephen and others.
	Easter	Visits Greece and Constantinople with Keynes.
	June	Exhibits at an exhibition of the Friday Club, Alpine Club Gallery. Attends the first Post-Impressionist exhibition at the Grafton Gallery.
	Winter	Exhibits with the New English Art Club.
1911	Easter	Visits Tunis and Sicily with Keynes. Exhibits at least one work in the Friday Club exhibition.
	Summer	Paints *Football* and *Bathing* as part of the decoration of the Borough Polytechnic dining-room; other painters participating were Bernard Adeney, Frederick Etchells, Roger Fry, Max Gill and Albert Rutherston.
	November	With Keynes moves to 38 Brunswick Square, house of Adrian and Virginia Stephen.
	December	As a member of the Camden Town Group exhibits *Tulips* (bought by Edward Marsh) at Camden Town Group exhibition.
1912		Paints with Etchells a mural in Keynes's rooms at Brunswick Square, and by himself paints mural in Adrian Stephen's room and part of the mural in the hall of Roger Fry's house, Durbins, near Guildford.
	February	Represented by two paintings at the Friday Club exhibition.
	July	Represented by six paintings in the 'Exposition de Quelques Indépendants Anglais', Galerie Barbazanges, Paris.

	October–December	Six works shown in the English section of the second Post-Impressionist exhibition. *The Queen of Sheba* bought by Roger Fry who shortly afterwards sells it to the Contemporary Art Society.
		Designs costumes for proposed *Macbeth* for Granville-Barker (play not produced).
1913	March	Shows with the Grafton Group (other members Fry, Vanessa Bell, Wyndham Lewis and Etchells), at the Alpine Club Gallery, an exhibition in which pictures are shown anonymously without titles.
		Becomes a co-director (with Vanessa Bell) of the Omega Workshop. Associated with the Omega until its closure in 1919.
	Second half	Commissioned by Clive Bell to paint *Adam and Eve* for the Contemporary Art Society.
		Designs costumes for production of *Twelfth Night* by Jacques Copeau at Vieux Colombier, Paris. Staged in May 1914 with success.
1914		With Roger Fry and Vanessa Bell, paints mural decorations for Henry Harris in Bedford Square and Ethel Sands in Chelsea.
	May–June	Represented by five paintings at the twentieth-century art exhibition at Whitechapel Art Gallery.
	June	Exhibits six works at Grafton Group second exhibition.
	Second half	Executes non-representational designs on a roll of paper (now in the Tate Gallery), designed as a kinetic work to move to an accompaniment of music by Bach.
1915	*c.* April–May	Paints non-representational picture in memory of Rupert Brooke.
	June	Exhibits by invitation at the Vorticist exhibition two constructions and one other work.

1916	Early	Together with David Garnett, Vanessa Bell and others, addresses envelopes for the National Council for Civil Liberties in connection with conscription.
	c. March–September	Together with David Garnett rents and works a fruit farm, Wissett Lodge, near Halesworth, Suffolk.
	Summer	Given status of conscientious objector. Ordered to work on land.
	September–October	Together with Vanessa Bell and David Garnett moves to Charleston near Firle, Sussex.
	From September	Working full-time in agriculture. Develops rheumatism.
1917	Summer	Designs costumes for Copeau's production in New York of *Pelléas et Mélisande*.
	October	Represented by nine works at 'The New Movement in Art' exhibition, Mansard Gallery, London.
1917 1918	October – November	Working part-time in agriculture.
1918	February–March	Obtains catalogue of Degas sale: suggests to Keynes that nation should make purchases. As a result, works by Ingres, Corot, Delacroix, Forain, Gauguin, Manet and others bought for the National Gallery.
	May–June	Grant suggested as war artist, to paint on subject of 'allotments' for proposed Hall of Memory, but impossibility of release from agricultural work prevents implementation of plan.
	August	Represented at the 'Moderne Englische Malerei' exhibition at the Kunsthaus, Zurich.
	Soon after Armistice	Discontinues agricultural work.
	Christmas Day	Birth of Angelica Bell, daughter of Vanessa Bell and Duncan Grant.

1919		Member of the London Group.
	April–May	Exhibits at the tenth exhibition of the London Group.
	November	Exhibits at the eleventh exhibition of the London Group.
1920		Takes studio at 8 Fitzroy Street.
	February	First one-man exhibition at the Carfax Gallery, London.
	Easter	Visits Rome with Vanessa Bell and Keynes.
1921	November	Exhibits watercolours at the Independent Gallery, Grafton Street, in company with Robert Lotiron and Vanessa Bell.
1922		Finishes decorations with Vanessa Bell for Keynes's rooms in Webb's Building, King's College, Cambridge.
1923		Second one-man exhibition at the Independent Gallery.
1925		Designs decor for ballet *The Postman* at the Coliseum. Decorates with Vanessa Bell, Moon Hall, Gomshall, Surrey, the house of Peter Harrison.
1926		Represented at the XV Biennale, Venice.
	May–June	Exhibits at the Leicester Galleries with the London Artists' Association; Bernard Adeney, Keith Baynes, Vanessa Bell, Frank Dobson, Roger Fry and F.J. Porter.
c. 1926–8		Executes with Vanessa Bell decorations in the house of Mr and Mrs St J. Hutchinson, Regent's Park.
1927		Exhibits with the London Artists' Association. With Vanessa Bell executes decorations at Château d'Aupegard, near Offranville, for Miss Sands and Miss Hudson.
1927–38	Summer	Regular visits to Cassis, near Marseilles.

1929	February–March	Retrospective exhibition (1910–29) at Paul Guillaume and Brandon Davis Ltd, 73 Grosvenor Street, London.
1929–31		Member of the London Artists' Association.
1930		With Vanessa Bell decorates Penns-in-the-Rocks, Withyham, Sussex, for Lady Gerald Wellesley.
1931	June–July	Exhibition of recent paintings, London Artists' Association, Cooling Galleries.
	November–December	Included in 'Recent Pictures by British Artists' exhibition, Agnew & Sons.
1932		Represented at the XVIII Biennale, Venice, in the official British pavilion.
	June–July	Exhibits in 'Recent Paintings by Duncan Grant, Vanessa Bell and Keith Baynes', Agnew & Sons.
1932–9		Textile designs produced for Allan Walton.
1933	June	'Drawings by Duncan Grant' exhibition, Agnew & Sons.
1934	November–December	Exhibition 'Gainsborough to Grant', Agnew & Sons.
1935		RMS *Queen Mary* decorations commissioned by the Cunard-White Star Steamship Company, and rejected the following year.
1937	June–July	Coronation exhibition, 'Contemporary British Artists', Agnew & Sons.
	November–December	'Recent Works by Duncan Grant' exhibition, Agnew & Sons.
1938		Teaches at Euston Road School.

127

1940	May–June	Represented by 33 paintings intended for the **XXII** Biennale, Venice. This consignment never sent but shown at the Wallace Collection.
	Summer	In Plymouth as official war artist.
1940–3		Carries out decorations for the parish church at Berwick, near Firle, Sussex, in collaboration with Vanessa Bell and her son Quentin.
1944		*Cinderella* decorations by Duncan Grant and Vanessa Bell for the Children's Restaurant, Tottenham, unveiled by Lord Keynes.
1945	June–July	One-man exhibition of recent paintings at the Leicester Galleries.
1946	July	First meets Paul Roche and asks him to model.
	August	Travels with his mother to Copenhagen and sketches.
1946–8		Takes a room in Miss Marjorie Strachey's flat in Taviton Street, off Gordon Square.
1948–56		Takes a flat in Canonbury overlooking Canonbury Square.
1956		Takes a room at 28 Percy Street, Tottenham Court Road. Designs decor for the English Opera Group's production of John Blow's *Venus and Adonis*, first performed at the Aldeburgh Festival, 15 June.
1957	May	Exhibition of paintings, Leicester Galleries.
1958		Decorates the Russell Chantry, Lincoln Cathedral, using Paul Roche as the model for Christ.
1959	May–June	Retrospective exhibition at the Tate Gallery (Arts Council).

1962		Rents top flat at 24 Victoria Square from Leonard Woolf.
1964	November	'Duncan Grant and His World' retrospective exhibition at Wildenstein & Co. Ltd.
1966		'Paintings by Duncan Grant and Vanessa Bell' exhibition at the Royal West of England Academy, Bristol.
	Summer	Painting in Morocco.
1967	June–August	Twenty-seven works in 'Artists of Bloomsbury' exhibition, the Rye Art Gallery, Sussex.
1968	Summer	Takes a studio in Fez, Morocco, for two months.
1969		Visits Holland.
	November–December	'Portraits by Duncan Grant', Arts Council exhibition (with tour) at the Arts Council Gallery, Cambridge.
1970		Visits Paris and Cyprus. Moves to 3 Park Square West, London. Awarded honorary doctorate, Royal College of Art.
1972	January–February	Visits Portugal. Awarded honorary doctorate, University of Sussex.
	April–May	Watercolours and drawings exhibition, Anthony d'Offay Gallery.
1973	January	Exhibition at the Fermoy Gallery, King's Lynn. The Queen Mother buys *Still Life with Matisse*.
	September	Flies with Paul Roche to Turkey. Visits Istanbul, Antalya, Side, Kemer and many Greco-Roman sites.
1974	August	Drives with Paul Roche through Scotland. Visits his birthplace.

1975	January	Reaches the age of ninety. Exhibitions celebrating the event at Scottish National Gallery of Modern Art; Museum of Modern Art, Oxford; Tate Gallery; Towner Art Gallery, Eastbourne; Anthony d'Offay Gallery; Gallery Edward Harvane; Davis and Long Gallery, New York.
	October	Travels with Paul Roche to Tangier and lives in Rex Nan Kivell's house, 'El Farah'. Nursed by Paul Roche through nearly terminal pneumonia.
1976	May	Returns to England. Exhibition of paintings and drawings at Southover Gallery, Lewes, largely of work done in Tangier.
1977	April	Exhibition at the Rye Art Gallery; much of the work done in Tangier during 1975–6.
	October	Moves from Charleston to The Stables, The Street, Aldermaston (Roche household).
1978	April	Flies with Paul Roche to Paris to see exhibition 'The Last Ten Years of Cézanne'; guest of the British Embassy. Returns to Aldermaston. Paints his last picture: a small flower-piece.
	May 9th*	Dies in Aldermaston of bronchial pneumonia. Buried next to Vanessa Bell in Firle churchyard.
	June 27th	Memorial service in St Paul's Cathedral.
1981	November–December	'Works on Paper' exhibition, Anthony d'Offay Gallery.

----

* *The Times* obituary mistakenly gave the date of Duncan's death as May 8th.

INDEX